American Manufacturing 2.0

American Manufacturing 2.0

What Went Wrong and How to Make It Right

Steven L. Blue

Foreword by Bill McDermott

 PRAEGER™

An Imprint of ABC-CLIO, LLC

Santa Barbara, California • Denver, Colorado

Library of Congress Cataloging-in-Publication Data

Names: Blue, Steven L., author.
Title: American manufacturing 2.0 : what went wrong and how to make
    it right / Steven L. Blue.
Description: Santa Barbara : Praeger, 2016. | Includes bibliographical
    references and index.
Identifiers: LCCN 2016016773 | ISBN 9781440838705 (hardback) |
    ISBN 9781440838712 (ebook)
Subjects: LCSH: Manufacturing industries—Government policy—United States. |
    Manufacturing industries—United States.
Classification: LCC HD9726 .B58 2016 | DDC 338.4/7670973—dc23
LC record available at https://lccn.loc.gov/2016016773

ISBN: 978–1–4408–3870–5
EISBN: 978–1–4408–3871–2

20 19 18 17 16   2 3 4 5

This book is also available as an eBook.

Praeger
An Imprint of ABC-CLIO, LLC

ABC-CLIO, LLC
130 Cremona Drive, P.O. Box 1911
Santa Barbara, California 93116-1911
www.abc-clio.com

This book is printed on acid-free paper ∞

Manufactured in the United States of America

Contents

Foreword

One of the most powerful things leaders can do is incite change before change is absolutely necessary. For America's manufacturers, the time to incite change is now.

In the United States, manufacturing is amidst a comeback. Outsourcing abroad continues to be less cost effective and the desirability of Made in America tugs production back home. The question U.S.-based manufacturers are asking is how can they capitalize on this shift.

The most consequential change manufacturers can undertake, however, involves a very different type of machinery than what already resides on the shop floor. I refer to the machinery of people, the internal gears that make customers and employees tick. This is why the largest factor determining whether your company wins amidst manufacturing's resurgence will be the quality of its leadership.

Today, manufacturing needs more leaders of consequence.

Leaders of consequence influence people's emotions, minds, and actions to produce measurable results for individuals as well as organizations. This ability is science as well as art, and it is in short supply. While innovative products and processes will continue to be the bread-and-butter of high performing organizations, culture will, perhaps more than ever, be the secret sauce. That is because unlike machines and techniques, culture—as author Steven Blue insightfully emphasizes—is impossible to replicate.

Shortsighted thinkers, hopefully your competition, dismiss "culture" as too soft or immeasurable, and not worthy of investment. They have already put down this book. The long-sighted leader, the leader that wants to build a sustainable business, knows that every company and every team has a culture, whether or not it is purposeful. An environment is either toxic or healthy. Wasteful or productive. Dispiriting or inspiring. Leaders of consequence understand that they are in a position to choose.

Reading *American Manufacturing 2.0* is a first step in that journey.

Values, Steve understands, are the building blocks of culture. Leaders not only choose the values that matter to them, but their actions determine whether those values are adhered to or ignored. The key values that *American Manufacturing 2.0* focuses on provide an excellent roadmap based on Steve's own experience as a CEO—and as a leader of consequence.

Values, of course, are also personal, so I humbly suggest two additional values to the foundation Steve has so beautifully set. To his list I add empathy and trust.

In my five decades of building businesses—from a corner store in New York to my current role as a global CEO of the world's largest business software company, SAP—empathy and trust have served my customers, my employees, and served me. These are bedrock values from which I try to lead today.

Empathy is about getting out of your own head, ignoring ego, and getting into the heads and the hearts of others—especially customers and employees. Listen to people's desires and feel their pain. Only when you understand others' problems can you offer simple solutions. Only when you know others' goals can you come up with better ways to achieve them.

For your customers, and for your customers' customers, empathy allows you to make products that the market truly loves to consume. Today, with innovation happening at such high speeds, empathy is the low-tech tool of choice because it allows us to envision what customers want and need before they demand it. High-tech tools plucked from our digital environs give empathy new life by helping to capture and track desires and behaviors. Leaders who constantly imagine the perfect user experience, encourage their colleagues to do the same, and follow up by acknowledging and acting on those imaginings, are nurturing a culture of empathy.

The future of manufacturing also brings with it a new war for talent. The most experienced workers, those in their fifties and older, will soon leave the workforce. In their wake is a pool of younger talent with different expectations and definitions of success. To recruit and retain the best people, even manufacturers must understand this growing cohort if they are to harness their skills and win their loyalty. Leaders of consequence must get to know people young and old beyond their titles and see them as human beings with incredible potential to exceed expectations, motivated by purpose as well as a paycheck.

Only once you show an unwavering commitment to your people, and prove you care about their successes as much as your own, can you hold employees accountable to the high expectations required for manufacturers to win in the evolving marketplace. Accountability without empathy demotivates people. The alternative yields unwavering loyalty.

My second bedrock value is trust because it truly is the ultimate currency. Trust earns followers and ignites hard, impassioned work. Leaders of consequence trust people to understand their vision and execute their piece of it. In turn, leaders of consequence are trusted to deliver a compelling yet achievable vision. Embedded in any vision must be the best interests of the organization. As a pillar of a healthy culture, trust takes a long time to establish but can be destroyed in a moment. Trust is yours to earn, every day.

Empathy, trust, and the other core values in *American Manufacturing 2.0* cannot be measured, which makes them easy targets to dismiss. These values also cannot be ordered online and delivered in hours. They take time, often years, to take hold—which is another reason the shortsighted leader dismisses them. But when values are lacking everyone notices and organizations suffer in ways that even an economic resurgence cannot mask. For this reason, cultural change built on a bedrock of values must begin as soon as you put this book down. Better yet, as you turn the pages.

A leader's legacy is based on more than financial success. Your legacy will be defined by how many people's lives you touch along the way, and the good feelings and memories that linger long after you have gone. Only a company culture that leverages human interaction as a competitive advantage ensures success for you, your customers, and your organization for years to come.

Let the reading, and the journey, begin.

Bill McDermott
Chief Executive Officer, SAP

Introduction

During most of the twentieth century, if you wanted something made well—an automobile, telephone, child's toy, paper clip—the best choice was to manufacture it in America. The United States offered state-of-the-art factories, skilled labor, cheap energy, robust markets, and all the other ingredients that together created the world's leading manufacturing powerhouse.

Then something happened. As we turned the corner to a new century, our manufacturing prowess faded. Seemingly overnight, competitors in China, Mexico, and other developing nations started getting the contracts and shipping the goods. While their factories produced items that were once made in the United States, our factories were shuttered and our workers laid off. Today, if you walk through any consumer retail store and pick an item off the shelf, the odds are high that the label will read "Made in China."

This is not an academic issue of interest only to business school programs. The decline of manufacturing in America has brought job loss and income stagnation, and it has slammed shut the door that once led to middle-class stability and comfort for millions. Without a robust manufacturing sector, it is that much more difficult for the average American to achieve the American dream. The middle class is under siege, and Americans feel it in their pocketbooks. It is a real problem that has real-life consequences for our nation.

This book offers a new vision for the future.

American Manufacturing 2.0 lays out a road map for a renewal of this vital industry. I believe that there is no reason why we should accept our current state of affairs. To think of a resurgence of manufacturing in America is not science fiction. It is reality, and this book will show you how and where it is happening today, and how it can grow stronger in the future. Current indicators foresee the potential for a bright future for the American industrial manufacturing sector, but only if we seize the opportunity to reemerge as a global manufacturing power.

This book is about the journey manufacturers can take, where we have gone wrong, and where we need to go if we want to get back to the top. *American Manufacturing 2.0* offers hands-on, practical advice and insights from the front lines of the industry. It was not written by a historian, strategist, consultant, or business school professor. It was written by an experienced industry insider who respects the heritage and history of America's great and mighty industrial manufacturing sector.

My message—whether you are a CEO, executive, employee, policy maker, professor, or a young person considering which career to choose —is that the time is now or never. No one will do it for us. Not the government and certainly not our competitors. As American manufacturers, we need to do it ourselves.

THE POWER OF INGENUITY

This book is aimed primarily at small to mid-sized manufacturing companies that survive by their wits and by hard work. Every American should salute these warriors for our nation's economy! They are the front-line troops in the war to keep America great.

My message is that to survive and thrive, small manufacturers cannot take anything for granted. We must set our sights higher, and expect more from ourselves and our employees.

For example, too many small manufacturing companies accept single-digit earnings as a percentage of sales.

When I ask the leaders of embattled manufacturing companies why they are not earning double digits, they often rationalize their performance with statements like, "We perform on a level with our peers," or "We're right on track with the average profits in our industry."

These companies are anemic and do not even know it. They are in the middle of a crisis that will engulf them in the global war of the business worlds. Worse, they may be headed for a turnaround and do not know that either! By the time they realize they need a turnaround, it will probably be too late. If they come out on the other side at all, they will not ever be the same.

"That's not my company," you say. "We're doing okay."

Very well—if you do not want to set your sights higher, and if you want to hear only soothing platitudes, then please pass this book to the next person. It is not for you.

On the other hand, if you want to play to win, this book is for you. If you are looking for corporate tough love, you have come to the right place.

Still with me? Good! Let's find out how well you are *really* doing. The following symptoms of a manufacturing company headed for oblivion are clear and unmistakable. You will know if your company has any of them.

Do your senior managers play the "I can't control game"? You know what I mean: Sales cannot control when manufacturing makes the product. Manufacturing cannot control the promises sales makes. Product development cannot control what manufacturing does. I will bet your whole company plays this game. And you want to know the worst part? You go along with it. Sound familiar?

Speaking of your senior leaders, whose team do they play on? Your sales executives probably play solely on the sales team. Your manufacturing people play on the manufacturing team. Quality owes its allegiance to the quality function. Everybody's doing their jobs, right? Do not forget, everyone was doing their job when the Titanic went down too.

What about manufacturing? Is your cost of sales going down significantly every single year? Or do you buy into the "we can't do anything about costs" argument? Hmm, I thought so.

Every person in your company needs to be one of three things: a superstar, a soon-to-be superstar, or a soon-to-be ex-employee. When you talk about superstars, do your human resources people tell you this scenario is not practical?

Let's try something a little easier. Who is responsible for profit in your company? If you are the CEO, are you the only one responsible? Or is *everyone* accountable for profit?

Your salespeople work for the customer, not your company, right? Do you buy the sales argument that "the customer pays the bills"?

Does it appear that things just do not seem to get done in your company? Do you hear an endless string of reasons why more progress is not made? Does there seem to be a lot of activity but few results?

Does your company have a culture by default, rather than one that you have purposefully designed?

These are the symptoms of most single-digit-earnings (as a percentage of sales) companies. In most middle-market manufacturers, earnings in the double digits are the exception rather than the rule.

My goal is to help you make your company the exception.

ALL ABOARD THE INNOVATION EXPRESS!

You do not have to plod along every day, fearing a takeover, fearing China, fearing politicians, fearing unions! I know what this feels like, and I can help you rise above it. I have taken small, rustbelt, low-technology businesses and transformed them into double-digit-earning global powerhouses. And I am talking 20 percent—and more—earnings as a percentage of sales.

I have built teams that launched blizzards of industry-first products, changed cultures from worst-in-class to best-in-breed, and created global alliances from vaporware.

You can too.

I learned how to do this the hard way. I lived through the worst management nightmare you can imagine in a turnaround: deciding whether to pay the electricity bill or payroll, caught between militant unions and unreasonable absentee foreign shareholders, negotiating unlikely-to-succeed deals. I had bricks thrown through my living room window and was forced to agree to unjustifiable objectives just to make the boss look good. I attended sixteen-hour marathon meetings, day after day, where nothing was done but pass the blame—using any excuse we could think of just to get out of the room alive. Despite these challenges, I created a winning team that was the envy of the industry. Just another day in the life of a turnaround!

I also learned how to do this the *fun* way: taking terrific businesses and making them spectacular, creating unheard of sales-per-employee numbers, doubling sales and quadrupling profit. Just another day in the life of a company that acts like it needs a turnaround.

It was with these experiences that I discovered the path to the elite world of double-digit earnings and the rebirth of American industrial manufacturing in the twenty-first century. I developed The 7 Values of Ingenuity™ in over 40 years of trial and error, which you will learn about in this book. If you apply them, they can help you turn your company around, one idea at a time. I have also included real-life stories and exclusive interviews from the front lines—stories of leaders just like you who have overcome challenges and defied the trends to make their manufacturing companies shining beacons of success in the dim world of industrial decline.

I am grateful that you have picked up this book. I hope that the advice and experience I present will help you strengthen your company and make it a part of the great rebirth of American manufacturing.

Ready? Let's get started!

ONE

The Rise and Fall of American Manufacturing

It is an ordinary day. You wake up and turn off your alarm clock. You use a toothbrush to clean your teeth. You put bread into your toaster for breakfast. You drive yourself to work in your car.

In an industrialized society like the United States, you don't think twice about these everyday items—and thousands more—that make your life easier. You might even take them for granted. They seem so simple and so obvious. What could be so hard about making a ballpoint pen that is just the same as the other dozen ballpoint pens on your desk?

In reality, it is very hard. It takes determination, passion, and know-how to precisely manufacture even a simple item like a ballpoint pen, not to mention something like a highly complex jet aircraft with its 2 million parts.

Manufacturing—that is, using machinery to make something on a large scale—is such an advanced undertaking that human beings have been doing it for only the past 250 years of our 200,000-year history on this planet. In terms of our earthly existence, manufacturing is something that is still relatively new, and something that we can always get better at.

Manufactured goods—paper clips, smart phones, tennis shoes, automobiles, railroad cars, jet airliners—are produced so that each individual item has a high level of uniformity. When you buy one M10-150 metric hex nut at your local hardware store, you have every expectation of being able to buy 10,000 more of them that are indistinguishable from the first one you bought. And cheaply, too—these hex nuts are not pounded out one by one by your neighborhood blacksmith; they are made in huge quantities by machines.

Uniformity implies a widespread level of acceptance and usage, with lots of people using the same exact hex nut or driving the same car. You could argue that manufacturing is not absolutely necessary for human existence, and in fact throughout history, people have made some pretty cool stuff without the benefit of manufacturing. The Great Sphinx of Egypt was not manufactured. When Michelangelo painted the Sistine Chapel ceiling, it was not an exercise in manufacturing. Although some of its ubiquitous components were manufactured, the Apollo 11 spacecraft that brought man to the Moon was built by hand, one carefully fitted part at a time.

A society that is capable of producing individual works of art or unique projects, however, does not necessarily have what manufacturing makes possible, which are measurable physical benefits to large numbers of people. Manufacturing means improving the lives, in a uniform way, of a large population. Sometimes a single product can change an entire civilization. In the early twentieth century, the Ford Model T emerged as the first complex mass-produced machine in history, and its astoundingly rapid adoption by consumers changed the face of America. More recently, products such as the iPhone and its many competitors have changed the way people communicate on a global scale.

Only a true Luddite would assert that manufacturing has not been an amazing force for advancing human good. The manufacturing of the things we need has transformed the human race and shaped the world we live in today.

This raises an interesting question. If manufacturing is so good, then why doesn't everybody do it?

Why is the manufacturing of consumer and industrial goods not done in every nation, on every continent, all the time? And why do some nations, at various times in history, excel at manufacturing, while others lag behind?

To begin to find the answer, let's go back to the very dawn of manufacturing.

THE INDUSTRIAL REVOLUTION

Most historians agree that modern manufacturing—by which we mean the mass production of consumer goods—began during the Industrial

Revolution. At the end of the eighteenth century and the beginning of the nineteenth century, the making of consumer and industrial items quickly evolved from the hand production of goods—at first, primarily textiles—to their mass production with the aid of powered machines. This movement began in Great Britain, and within a few decades spread to Western Europe and North America.

Why did the Industrial Revolution begin in England, and not in Germany? Or China, or Japan?

Here's one explanation, offered in 1835 by Edward Baines in his book, *The History of the Cotton Manufacture in Great Britain*:

> The political and moral advantages of this country, as a seat of manufacturers, are not less remarkable than its physical advantages. The arts are the daughters of peace and liberty. In no country have these blessings been enjoyed in so high degree, or for so long a continuance, as in England. Under the reign of just laws, personal liberty and property have been secure; mercantile enterprise has been allowed to reap its reward; capital has accumulated in safety; the workman has "gone forth to his work and to his labour until the evening"; and, thus protected and favoured, the manufacturing prosperity of the country has struck its roots deep, and spread forth its branches to the ends of the earth.

He makes some good points, chief among them that manufacturing, which thrives on long-range planning, takes root in relatively stable societies that offer "political and moral advantages."

The more closely you look at England in the late eighteenth century, the more the Industrial Revolution begins to look inevitable. The reasons are myriad and sometimes unexpected—a finely balanced web of interrelated factors that combined to form a "perfect storm" of progress.

You might not think about this, but the availability of food played a factor.

During the seventeenth and eighteenth centuries, farmers in England were considered among the most productive worldwide. They investigated different varieties of vegetables and grains and strived to achieve greater yields through the use of new farming techniques. One of the new inventions by Jethro Tull was a mechanical seeder and horse-drawn hoe that allowed seeds to be automatically planted in consistent rows.

In England, high agrarian productivity and lower food prices meant more money was available to spend on consumer goods.

Across the Channel, conditions were very different. English society was far more open than in France, where there were onerous labor obligations to the feudal lords. The English farmers could travel to sell their goods, while the French farmers were bound by taxes, tariffs, and social restrictions.

Money makes a difference, too. Unlike France, England had a well-developed credit market and an effective central bank. Their government encouraged innovative technology and a free market with few restrictions on the management of the domestic economy.

If you are going to manufacture lots of stuff, you need consumers. During the century, the population in England nearly doubled, creating increased pressure to produce more consumer goods.

The industry that first emerged in England was the manufacture of a basic staple product, cotton textiles. This growth was the result of many pressure points and opportunities. For example, in the emerging textile industry there was an endless shortage of thread until Richard Arkwright invented a spinning device in 1765, which he called the water frame. At almost the same time, a carpenter named James Hargreaves invented the cotton jenny. These two discoveries produced 10 times more cotton yarn in 1790 than ever possible 20 years before.

The conditions for successful manufacturing existed first in England and nowhere else. Once it worked there, other highly organized societies—France, Germany, and the United States—hopped on the bandwagon and launched their own manufacturing enterprises, often by blatantly stealing ideas from the British.

MANUFACTURING COMES TO AMERICA

In the United States, Samuel Slater, a British expatriate, was known as the "Father of the American Industrial Revolution" and the "Father of the American Factory System." Born in England, he learned textile machinery firsthand as an apprentice to a pioneer in the British industry. In 1789, he came to the former colonies, and four years later built America's first successful water-powered roller spinning textile mill in Pawtucket, Rhode Island. In the land of his birth they called him "Slater the Traitor" because he brought British textile technology to America, creating new overseas competition for his old employers.

The United States, it turned out, was a terrific place for manufacturing to thrive. And thrive it did. In the decades following the Civil War, the United States emerged as an industrial giant. New industries emerged including steel manufacturing, petroleum refining, and electrical power.

These were endeavors pursued by men of vision who acted boldly and demanded nothing but success. Industrial growth transformed American society, producing a new class of wealthy industrialists, a prosperous middle class, and an expanded blue-collar working class. Millions of people who were born in the late eighteenth century witnessed a radical change in industrial transformation that profoundly changed not only where they worked but also where they lived. Millions of farmers migrated from their rural American agricultural roots to live and work in the rapidly expanding cities.

Manufacturing changed nearly every facet of American life, and its economic effects were massive. To use just one sector as representative of the totality, let's look at the railroad industry.

It all began in 1826, when Massachusetts incorporated the nation's first railroad system, the Granite Railway, as a common freight carrier for the purpose of hauling granite for the construction of the Bunker Hill Monument.

Other railroads authorized by states quickly followed suit, and in the following years new railroads included the Mohawk and Hudson, Delaware and Hudson Canal, and the Baltimore and Ohio Railroads.

To get started, Americans borrowed British railroad technology, and the first steam locomotives were used by the South Carolina Canal and Railroad Company.

To support its rapid growth, the B&O quickly got into manufacturing. In 1829, Mount Clare Shops opened in Baltimore to begin manufacturing railroad cars, locomotives, and iron bridges. Nevertheless, American railroad companies still imported much of their technology from Britain, particularly strap iron rails. In the mid-1840s, heavy iron "T" rails, which were more reliable and allowed for faster train speeds, were first manufactured in the United States at Mount Savage, Maryland and Danville, Pennsylvania. In the mid-nineteenth century, the manufacture of better quality rails was possible due to superior iron ores that were discovered, mainly in the Great Lakes area.

Iron rails were replaced with steel and were first made available in 1867 in Johnstown at the Cambria Iron Works.

Following the example set by B&O, American railroad companies soon began manufacturing their own equipment and thousands of domestic machine shops created products while thousands of tinkerers and inventors improved their inventions.

Railroads conquered untamed lands, connected the Atlantic to the Pacific, and brought the bold whistle of the passenger train to small towns and big cities alike. By 1880, the largest employer in the nation, aside from agriculture, was the U.S. rail industry, boasting 23,600 tons of freight being hauled by 17,800 locomotives, plus 22,200 passenger locomotives. The rapid growth of American railways had many effects including lower costs for food and all goods, the opening of hundreds of millions of acres of fertile farm land ready for development, a huge national sales market, the creation of the modern system of management, and the creation of a culture of engineering excellence.

THE PULLMAN COMPANY

Just as manufacturing companies can grow and become mighty, they can also decline and even perish. Perhaps no individual company symbolizes the heights to which American manufacturing rose, and then the depths to which it fell, more than the Pullman Company. Between the late nineteenth and early twentieth centuries, in the history of America's rail supply business, Pullman was the single, most important company and one of the world's leading manufacturers of railcars. Created by George M. Pullman, most of the railcars were made in Michigan and New York, and in the 1880s, a new plant was built south of Chicago. By 1890, Pullman was employing around 5,500 people who produced nearly 1,800 passenger cars and 12,500 freight cars a year. In the 1920s, Pullman Standard Car Manufacturing Company was producing hundreds of passenger cars and nearly 100,000 freight cars annually. If you rode in a passenger railcar, and especially if you traveled in a luxurious overnight sleeper, you probably rode in a Pullman.

Other firms manufactured specialized freight cars such as refrigerator cars, which transformed the meatpacking industry; tank cars, which were used to transport oil or other liquids; and cars such as glass-lined milk tank cars and nickel-lined compartments for holding acids. Factories churned out hundreds of thousands of specialty parts including lamps and lanterns; railroad track equipment such as crossings, switches, wheels, and brake beams.

With the rise of airlines and highways, the passenger train industry declined. In 1956, the last sleeping car rolled off the Pullman-Standard line, and in 1965 the last lightweight passenger car. The company continued to market and build cars for commuter rail and subway service and Superliners for Amtrak as late as the late 1970s and early 1980s. In 1981, Pullman-Standard was spun off from Pullman, Inc., as Pullman Technology, Inc., and was sold to Bombardier in 1987.

It was the end of an era.

But not the end of the railroad business, nor of railroad manufacturing. Across the continent, freight rail is still the mighty backbone of industrial transportation. There are good reasons for this. For long hauls of heavy loads, railroads can be four or five times as fuel efficient as trucks. The nation's 140,000 miles (224,792 km) of rail lines—double that of China's, the world's number two system in mileage—reach nearly every small town and large factory. According to the U.S. Department of Transportation, the freight rail system in the United States is the world's most dynamic network with 7 Class 1 railroads, 21 regional, and over 500 local railroads. With 1.3 million freight cars, the U.S. rail system moves more freight than any other freight rail system worldwide while providing over 200,000 jobs across the country. According to Markets and Markets, the value of the nation's rolling stock was estimated to be at $38.5 billion in 2014, and is projected to grow to $45.7 billion by 2019.

This vast industry requires manufacturing on a big scale. Which brings us around to the idea that manufacturing can, and must, evolve. While a mighty company like Pullman can fade with changing times, other companies—GE, Caterpillar, Bombardier, NRE—emerge to tackle the heavy manufacturing of railroad locomotives and rolling stock that meet the needs of today's demanding marketplace.

For anyone with a vested interest in manufacturing, the question is this: What does it take to create a successful manufacturing enterprise?

THE FIVE KEY CONDITIONS NEEDED FOR SUCCESSFUL MANUFACTURING

On both evolutionary and local levels, it is possible to identify those key environmental conditions that need to be present for manufacturing to thrive. Just as we saw in England during the dawn of the Industrial Revolution, and again in the United States during the period from after the Civil War to the 1970s, the convergence of just the right conditions can create the necessary environment for growth in manufacturing. If you don't have enough of these conditions in the right proportions, you are not going to have a good climate for manufacturing.

Here are the five key conditions that promote successful manufacturing within a society.

Markets That Are Free and Stable

Let's start by revisiting the words of Edward Baines, who wrote, "The arts are the daughters of peace and liberty." Manufacturing, and indeed nearly any economic enterprise, can flourish best in a climate where long-term planning is possible and where entrepreneurs are free to assert themselves in the marketplace. A nation where there is lawlessness is no more conducive to manufacturing than a nation that is choked by regulation and political oppression.

The presence of a strong government is not necessarily evil; it depends on what that government does. Based on the well-documented failures of state-controlled industry in the old Soviet Union, for example, you might conclude that any government involvement is bad. Economies that are controlled by central planning often perform poorly because governments are lousy at predicting future trends, there is a lack of incentive when your income is guaranteed, and governments tend to be inflexible and slow to respond to both shortages and surpluses.

But partnerships between the government and private industry can be potent. The United States proved this during World War II, when the manufacturing industry aligned with the federal government to create one of the biggest and most successful manufacturing partnerships in the history of the world. According to William S. Knudsen, a leading automotive industry executive during the war, "We won because we smothered the enemy in an avalanche of production, the like of which he had never seen, nor dreamed possible."

The massive effort impacted every sector of the U.S. manufacturing industry. For example, as the war heated up, U.S. aircraft manufacturers were turning out thousands of planes instead of their previous handful.

In 1939, total aircraft production for the U.S. military was less than 3,000 planes, which put us low on the list of major military powers. The American aircraft industry quickly adapted to the demands of war. Factories moved from one shift to two- and then three-shift schedules. The federal government encouraged development of skills and capacity by placing "educational orders" with manufacturers, and private firms used new government-built plants.

Cooperation among manufacturers was not only encouraged, but it was also required. Aircraft companies built planes designed by other manufacturers—for example, the B-17 was designed by Boeing and also built by Lockheed Vega and Douglas Aircraft. Automotive companies produced aircraft components and even complete aircraft. Ford restructured the massive Willow Run factory in order to build complete Consolidated B-24 Liberators, as well as sections of the plane to be assembled at other plants.

By the end of the war, America had produced an astonishing 300,000 planes of all types for its own Air Force and for its allies. It was the greatest air armada the world had ever seen, and every plane was made in America.

The Emergency Shipbuilding Program was the United States government's effort to quickly build durable cargo ships to carry troops and material overseas during the war. Managed by the U.S. Maritime Commission, the program built almost 6,000 cargo ships. Total U.S. naval ship production during the war included 27 aircraft carriers, 8 battleships, 48 cruisers, over 100 escort carriers, over 300 destroyers, and thousands of submarines, frigates, minesweepers, patrol boats, landing craft, and other vessels.

For the Army, American factories built nearly 70,000 armored tanks and 41,000 big guns and Howitzers. They churned out hundreds of thousands of utility vehicles—the everyday transports that keep an army on its feet. Take the humble Jeep; during the war, Willys produced 363,000 Jeeps and Ford about 280,000, for a total of over half a million of the ubiquitous lightweight vehicles. American factories also produced more than 800,000 military, 2½ ton trucks, and 7,500 railroad locomotives.

America consistently out-produced its enemies. By 1944, each American worker produced more than twice that of a German worker and four times the output of a Japanese worker. Commentators took this as proof that a democracy can outperform a totalitarian society; as Donald Douglas, the founder of the Douglas Aircraft Company observed, "Here's proof that free men can out-produce slaves."

When necessary, American manufacturing can ramp up to amazing levels. Whether in peacetime or at war, and regardless of your political affiliation, it is safe to conclude that over the past two centuries the United States has provided a safe and secure environment in which manufacturing companies can operate.

Raw Materials

It seems obvious to say this, but in order to make stuff, you need stuff. In our early days as a nation, the United States was a land of astonishingly abundant natural resources. We had endless forests of timber, deep quarries of granite, rolling fields of cotton, and mines bursting with gold, silver, tin, and iron ore. If you wanted to manufacture something, the chances were good that you could get the raw materials nearby. For things such as rubber and sugar you'd have to send your ships, but this was not an impossible task.

When Henry Ford ramped up production of the Model T, he had to secure huge quantities of raw materials. From 1910, when the Highland Park Plant opened, production doubled in each of the first three years, from 19,000 cars in 1910, to 34,500 in 1911, to an amazing 78,440 in 1912. The vast complex surrounding the Highland Park Plant included a power plant, machine shop, and foundry. To feed this enormous machine, by the 1920s Ford had purchased coal mines in Kentucky, a rubber plantation in Brazil, acres of timberland and iron-ore mines in Michigan and Minnesota, a fleet of ships, and a railroad. This vertical integration helped Ford ensure his company would have the necessary raw materials and parts, guaranteeing a continuously operating assembly line.

If you are short of raw materials—like Japan—and if you want to make a profit in manufacturing you have to offset the higher price for imported materials with a lower cost somewhere else, like in labor, or you need the benefit of a government subsidy.

Labor

If you want to manufacture something, you need people who will show up on time, who can do the job, and who care about the quality of their work. What your worker wants is a good wage, the respect of his or her employer, and the hope of climbing the economic and social ladder.

Over different periods of our history, the relationship between owners and labor has taken many forms. In the colonial era, American shop owners and guildsmen benefitted from the traditional apprentice system, which bound the employee to the employer by an enforceable contract. Benjamin Franklin was such an apprentice; to escape his contract at age sixteen he had to flee from Boston to Philadelphia, well beyond the reach of his former employer, who happened to be his own brother.

Landowners benefitted from the importation of cheap labor from Africa, in the form of slaves. English factory owners during the dawn of the Industrial Revolution also benefitted from the importation of slaves to the Americas, by virtue of the Triangle Trade.

The colonial Triangle Trade routes went from America to England, then to Africa, and then back to England. The goods that were shipped to England from the colonies included raw materials from American natural resources such as timber, fur, iron, fish, whale oil, sugar, tobacco, rice, and cotton. In addition, rum, which was one of the first American consumer products, was among the first finished goods that were sent to England.

England shipped textiles, beads and trinkets, iron products, ammunition, guns, and copper to Africa.

On the third leg of the triangle, Africa sent slaves (a key commodity) to America while ivory, spices, feathers, and gold were destined for Europe.

The Triangle Trade, coupled with the policy of Mercantilism, provided a bartering system so that gold and silver never had to leave England or the colonies to pay for purchases. England prospered the most in the trading since their finished goods were valued much higher than the raw resources from the colonies.

With the end of slavery in the North and the rise of the factory system, owners found cheap labor by hiring immigrants and children. Business owners needed reliable laborers who were willing to work up to twelve hours a day, six days a week. Immigrants from Ireland, Germany, Scandinavia, Italy, and other European countries flooded into the United States searching for employment. National child labor laws were not enacted until 1918, so immigrants often sought employment in factories because they could put their whole family to work. Factory owners supported child labor, asserting that it was good for everything from the economy to building the characters of the children. Parents of the children who worked had little choice because they needed the income.

Henry Ford was one of the first big factory owners to raise wages and consciously aim to develop a strong middle class of industrial workers. His motives were not entirely altruistic; he realized that if you pay fairly, your employee turnover rate goes down and productivity goes up. He paid his men well, but in return he demanded dedication and excellence.

This worked very well for Ford in the first half of the twentieth century; but if your labor costs get out of whack, you may have to make some painful adjustments.

Any book about American manufacturing is going to eventually get around to talking about the greatest case study of corporate mismanagement in history, which would be General Motors (GM). It is an axiom that one of the reasons for the unprofitability of GM during the decades leading up to its bankruptcy was its bloated labor costs. In 2009, GM reported that the total of both cash compensation and benefits provided to GM hourly workers in 2006 amounted to approximately $73.26 per active hour worked, including $39.68 in pay and $33.58 in benefits such as pensions, group life insurance, disability benefits, and supplemental unemployment benefits.

Meanwhile, for each Toyota car made in its U.S. plants the labor costs were only $48 per hour.

Healthcare was a big chunk of GM's labor costs. For instance, to make a vehicle cost the company $1,635 dollars on healthcare for active and retired workers in the United States, while Toyota paid only $215 per vehicle for active workers.

The flip side of the coin is that today's manufacturing jobs are becoming increasingly sophisticated, and workers with degrees in science, technology, engineering, and mathematics (STEM) are needed in ever-increasing numbers. They are worth more, and they get paid more than the guy who, fifty years ago, stood on the assembly line at the GM plant and spent eight hours a day tightening bolts.

Having emerged from the Great Recession, the U.S. economy could use more workers with STEM degrees, whether at the associate or bachelor's level. Wages have grown relatively quickly in many STEM-focused occupations, which is a clear indication of a shortage. Vacancies for STEM jobs are going unfilled in large numbers, and the median duration of advertising for STEM vacancies is more than twice that of those in other fields.

Energy

To undertake manufacturing on any scale, you need energy. The first sources of power for industry were the wind—like the windmills in the Netherlands—and water. In the Americas, the first industrial enterprises were built where running water could be channeled to turn a wheel, which powered a mill for grain.

The problems with using water as an energy source are that you have to situate your factory near a water source—a fast-moving river—and that your unpredictable water source can freeze in winter and dry up in summer.

During the nineteenth century, industry's increasing power demands led to innovations in existing steam engine technology.

George Henry Corliss, an American mechanical engineer and inventor, introduced his Corliss engine in 1849. Some of its advanced features, such as enhanced fuel efficiency, low maintenance, and superior power production, enabled thread to be produced at greater speed with less breakage, and in 1878 the engine was even used to pump the rivers of Pawtucket, Rhode Island. The efficiency of the Corliss also played an essential role in the expansion of the rail industry's large-scale production of steel rails.

In the twentieth century, America's extensive energy reserves included coal, petroleum, and natural gas. Electricity became widely available and reliable (even today, in some developing nations this is not necessarily the case). If you wanted to open a manufacturing facility in the United States, finding the energy to operate your machines was not your biggest problem.

Leadership

For manufacturing to succeed anywhere, at any time, perhaps the most important condition that must be fulfilled is the presence of strong leadership. We have seen this throughout history, from Samuel Slater to Henry Ford to Jack Welch: The captain of the ship can determine whether the voyage will be successful or end up on the rocks.

That is what this book is all about.

While factors such as free markets, raw materials, labor, and energy are not entirely within your control, your leadership is totally within your control. While you cannot control what factory workers are paid in China, or the price of gas for your delivery trucks, or the quality of the school system in your town, or what politicians in Washington are doing, you can —and must—control the example you set for your employees and your company.

In the pages that follow, I provide examples of companies that faced tremendous external challenges and which were turned around by the ingenuity of their leadership. They prove that at the end of the day, the old saying "where there's a will there's a way" is absolutely true. As we will see, while your competitors can buy the same machines as you and run the same ads for their products, none of them can copy your leadership and the culture of excellence that you establish in your company.

THE DECLINE OF MANUFACTURING IN AMERICA

These five key conditions are not the only ones needed for a culture of manufacturing, of course. You also need managers and inventors—people who have ideas and who know how to create new products. They need to have a strong work ethic and an unwavering commitment to excellence. You need consumers; after all, you can make the finest snowmobiles in Texas, but if no one needs one, you are not going to sell any. You need capital to fund your factory and buy materials. You need a good transportation system to get the raw materials to your factory and to ship your goods to market. You need a market where you can sell your goods.

By a fortuitous convergence of all these factors, from the turn of the twentieth century until the next century, no nation on earth was a bigger manufacturing powerhouse than the United States. Especially in the years following World War II, the United States had every condition needed for manufacturing success: a stable market environment, plenty of raw materials, a skilled and willing labor pool, and cheap energy. The United States also boasted a class of industrial leaders who were innovative, consumers who were ready to buy, access to capital, and a nationwide transportation system second to none.

As we entered the twenty-first century, the nation's manufacturing sector seemed to fall off a cliff. According to the Bureau of Labor Statistics, U.S. manufacturing employment fell from 19.6 million in 1979 to 13.7 million in 2007. More than half of this decline occurred in the years following the 2001 recession, with 1.5 million manufacturing jobs lost in the first year of that downturn and 900,000 jobs lost during the first year of the Great Recession.

What happened?

The reasons for the drop-off are exceedingly complex, and if you want to get into a good argument, just walk into any chamber of commerce meeting and present your personal theory.

The obvious reasons are the sudden availability of cheap, just-skilled-enough labor in China and other emerging nations, the relatively low cost of the global transport of goods, and the support given by foreign governments to their domestic manufacturing sectors. These conditions came together just at a time when U.S. labor was relatively expensive. Many U.S. firms did the math and figured out that they could manufacture their sneakers, clothing, refrigerators, and TV sets more cheaply overseas while maintaining the quality that American consumers expected.

China's currency manipulation and other protectionist practices benefitted its own export sector. China's brutal suppression of labor rights held down local wages, thus making outsourcing more cost efficient for U.S. companies.

Between 2001 (when China joined the WTO) and 2013, offshoring to China resulted in middle-class wage stagnation and the erosion of 3.2 million U.S. jobs; 75 percent within manufacturing.

When you look at the conditions that need to exist for viable manufacturing, it is clear that in the United States the near-perfect conditions that existed for a hundred years changed dramatically at the end of the twentieth century. The question is, when they return—which it seems as though they will—is American business going to be ready to reassert its primacy in manufacturing?

TWO

Manufacturing 2.0

In the first chapter I outlined the importance of manufacturing to our way of life, how it took root in Great Britain and then the United States, and how by the middle of the twentieth century the United States became the preeminent global leader in manufacturing. Then came the slow decline, the Great Recession, and then, in the past few years, the glimmer of real recovery.

I asked if manufacturing is so good, then why is it not being done all the time, in every nation? Why do some nations emerge as manufacturing centers, while others lag far behind? I revealed the five primary environmental conditions required to support robust manufacturing: free and stable markets, plentiful raw materials, good labor, accessible energy, and leadership. I also mentioned other important conditions, such as visionary inventors and an unwavering commitment to excellence shared by every member of the team.

With the environment ripe for U.S. manufacturing to become bigger than ever, I am on a crusade to revive American manufacturing and save American jobs. I do not want to see even one more American manufacturer get eviscerated by a foreign predator. I am dedicated to personally educating others in the industry on exactly how to fix bloated and broken companies, how to make good companies great, and how to make great companies greater. Until these lessons are learned and well employed, America will continue to lag amid burgeoning international threats.

While for any manufacturing industry to thrive in a particular nation you need the five requirements, I'd like to make it clear that right now, today, in the United States we have the conditions necessary for a resurgence of manufacturing success. We have what it takes for Manufacturing 2.0.

Yes, I hear all the negative talk promulgated by the naysayers.

Owners complain about the tax code. They assail U.S. corporate taxes as excessive and among the highest in the world. (And as a matter of fact, what they say is true.)

Workers' groups blast income and sales taxes for being disproportionately weighted against average income earners.

Everyone points their finger at China for ignoring trade agreements, India for exploiting its population as a cheap labor source, Organization of the Petroleum Exporting Countries (OPEC) and its allies for manipulating energy markets, Greece for dragging down Europe's economy, and South Americans for being corrupt. All of these complaints have shreds of merit.

But blaming international market conditions and lousy tax codes for poor performance is nothing more than a convenient excuse for failing companies. It is like blaming winter because it is cold.

If you are the CEO of a major international company like General Electric, or the head of a trade organization hired to lobby politicians in Washington, you can afford to be engaged in macroeconomic debates, like trade policy. You have the resources and the big corporate guns to have an influence. If you are a multinational computer technology corporation like Microsoft, trade agreements and tax policies do indeed directly impact your business and bottom line. But for most CEOs, myself included, there is not a damn thing we can do on our own about changing corporate tax codes, enforcing trade agreements with China, or combating cheap overseas labor costs. We swim in ponds, not oceans. Most of the competitive disadvantages we face are global, not local. They are intractable issues that will take many future presidents and legislators to resolve.

As CEO of a small-to-mid-sized company, your short-term viability depends on competing and winning on the playing field as it exists today, however hilly or unfair it may seem. And without short-term success, there is no long term.

Obviously, as chief executives, a part of our job is to be aware of what is happening around us and how events impact our businesses. If you sell parts to Microsoft, you are affected downstream. The price of oil certainly can hurt or help us, and we should anticipate swings in operating and material costs. But unless you are an OPEC member, or running Exxon Mobil, you are a passenger on that train—not the engineer or conductor. You need to know where the train is headed and then affect those things in your business that you can control. Global competition and high taxes are not reasons for failure. The best companies adjust and adapt no matter how hostile the marketplace.

Library shelves are full of books and academic papers dissecting the state of American manufacturing and the economy in general. It is easy to get down in the weeds with data and trying to construct—or even understand—economic trends. Some of the greatest minds in the world have spent lifetimes building predictive models. Many contradict one another.

One constant that I see in all of the business science is that *markets change*. They go boom or they go bust, and for lots of complex reasons. Knowing *why* these trends occur isn't as important as knowing that they *will* occur.

Look at our own economy. The business cycle comes and goes. And it comes and goes again. And each contraction is caused by a different set of circumstances or series of events, some foreseen and some not. Worrying about when the next bust cycle is going to strike is, to a large degree, a waste of time for people running smaller companies. The only certainty is that economic conditions *will change*. And the best hedge is to operate lean and smart all of the time. Create products that fix problems and hire the best workforce you can afford.

One of the best summaries I have seen that encapsulates the forces surrounding our manufacturing state, and business in general, was written in 2013 by Chad M. Moutray and Thomas Kevin Swift. It's called "Looking Ahead: Opportunities and Challenges for U.S. Manufacturers, Business Economics," in *Small Business Economics* (vol. 48, no. 2). At the time the study was published, Moutray was chief economist with the National Association of Manufacturers, and Swift was chief economist of the American Chemistry Council. Basically, these two economists rolled out a wealth of statistics suggesting that U.S. manufacturing is on the mend, but that we still have some structural challenges.

First, the good news. At the time of the study, industrial production had gone up almost 21 percent since the Great Recession. That is especially welcoming because, according to the authors, industrial manufacturers got clobbered during the massive downturn, shedding more than 2 million workers, which was about 17 percent of the total workforce. According to Moutray and Swift, the sectors within manufacturing that rebounded most were those most damaged in the decline. They included bedrock industries such as machinery, plastics and rubber products, motor vehicles, computers, and electronics. In the years ahead, opportunities include energy environment enhancement, an improvement in the international trade atmosphere, and progression in innovation. However, the sector must also contend with weakened growth in the global economy, onerous regulation and taxes, and an unprepared work force to manage the needs of the twenty-first century.

Given these external challenges, in my view the number one threat to Manufacturing 2.0 comes not from China or Washington. It comes from the corner office of your own company.

Why? It is because many CEOs of multimillion-dollar manufacturing companies are what I call "fat, dumb, and happy." In other words, a CEO who builds a company to a certain stage or takes over a company that is doing well, tends to become comfortable with where the company is now, and not necessarily concerned with where it could be in the years ahead.

This attitude is shortsighted. Companies are like water; they are meant to constantly be in motion. Leave water in a place where it is not moving and it becomes stagnant, diseased, and eventually deadly. Companies are the same way. *Change* is the word that needs to be carved over your doorway and posted on your wall. What works for you today may not work tomorrow. Once you think you've got the game figured out, the rules will change. Washington will issue new regulations. A new competitor will emerge. A new technology will render your product obsolete. Energy costs will rise. You name it, and it is going to happen—if not tomorrow, then the next day. If you are like a dinosaur that is oblivious to the meteor heading for earth, you've got a good chance of going extinct.

There are many aspects to staying ahead of the change wave that never stops coming at you. One happens to be the lean operations model that has transformed the companies that I have led. (In this book I am going to try to avoid tooting my own horn, but once in a while I am going to do it.)

Lean manufacturing (also known as lean production) originated from Toyota Production System's (TPS) renowned management philosophy on the reduction of Toyota's original "seven wastes" for the purpose of improving the customer's overall value. *Value* equates to a process or action that, from the client's perspective who uses the product or service, he or she would be prepared to pay for.

Lean also includes the practice of *kaizen*, Japanese and Chinese meaning "continuous improvement." Kaizen, when referring to the business, relates to actions that continuously advance and include everyone from the CEO to workers on the assembly line.

To be fair, Toyota refined what Henry Ford had started. In 1915, industrial engineering expert Charles Buxton Going wrote:

> Ford's success has startled the country, almost the world, financially, industrially, mechanically. It exhibits in higher degree than most persons would have thought possible the seemingly contradictory requirements of true efficiency, which are: constant increase of quality, great increase of pay to the workers, and repeated reduction in cost to the consumer. And with these appears, as at once cause and effect, an absolutely incredible enlargement of output reaching something like one hundredfold in less than ten years, and an enormous profit to the manufacturer.

Henry Ford's problem was that while his manufacturing process was amazingly efficient, it was not designed to cope with change. Eventually the Model T became obsolete, and the company's fortunes declined before it started producing the hugely successful Ford Model A in 1927.

Lean manufacturing is centered on emphasizing what adds value by reducing everything else. Entire textbooks have been written about lean manufacturing, but basically it means that if production flows in perfect response to consumer demand, then there is no inventory of unsold goods, and producing only the features that add customer value, simplifies the design, time and effort to create the product.

The objective of lean implementation is to reduce waste (*muda*), and remain flexible while operating within an ideal workflow that ensures the accuracy of moving products to the correct location, at the correct time, and in the correct quantity.

Lean also includes overburdening waste (*muri*) and workload waste (*mura*).

For example, the traditional way to make automobiles would be to forecast how many cars you would sell in a given period, such as a fiscal quarter, and with what features; and then you'd make those cars and deliver them to the showrooms. If you projected 10,000 cars were to be sold and by the end of the quarter you had sold only 9,500, you'd have 500 cars left over. On the other hand, if you had orders for 10,500 cars, you might actually lose sales because you couldn't deliver the extra 500 in time. Both scenarios represent costly inefficiencies.

The biggest nightmare on the showroom floor is when the customer walks in and says, "I love the car. It's perfect, and I can afford it. But the car you have is painted orange. I don't want orange; I want blue." The customer goes away, and you have a product with a feature—orange paint—that the customer doesn't want.

What if you had a car factory that could instantly produce the exact car the customer wants? That would be an ideal solution. The customer could say, "I want a blue car with this exact list of features," and you could say, "We'll have it for you tomorrow." The car wouldn't exist until the order had been placed.

Aside from some sales samples, there would be no inventory.

This is how print-on-demand books are made. If you go to Amazon and order a print-on-demand paperback book, the book will be printed, bound, and shipped upon receipt of your order. It will not be picked off the shelf from inventory. Print on demand means exactly that: The book is created only after it has been ordered.

While this is happening today with books, obviously we are not quite there yet with more complex manufactured products; but we are getting closer.

The partner of lean is "just in time." This means that instead of maintaining a warehouse full of the parts you need to build 10,000 cars, you either create or buy the parts "just in time" to use them on the assembly line. How many parts you need to keep on hand depends on the speed and reliability of your supply chain. In an ideal world, the customer would order the car, and instantly the parts for the car would be shipped to the factory to be assembled. To even attempt this kind of high-wire act requires a high level of responsiveness and transparency, and for that you need the very best people on your team.

Throughout this book, I am going to provide real-life stories of companies and CEOs who are a part of Manufacturing 2.0 right now. These bold industrialists are not accepting the status quo, and they do not believe the prophets of doom and gloom who assert that everything you buy at Walmart needs to be stamped "Made in China." These tough leaders set high standards for themselves and their employees, and they are proving that "Made in the U.S.A." is more than just a slogan from the good old days.

MANUFACTURING 2.0 ON THE RISE

As you will see in the pages ahead, there are many inspirational stories to give you hope that CEOs and managers are getting the message that this country's decline in manufacturing is reversible and that we can come out stronger than ever.

U.S. manufacturing is at a major turning point. The battles of quality and cost we had to fight in the 1980s against "Japan, Inc." are largely behind us. The huge manufacturing exodus to China is beginning to equalize itself; the Chinese are finding that success has its own inevitable costs, and American manufacturers are realizing that shipping their manufacturing to China and other developing nations may be a false economy.

Surveys continue to indicate that CEOs are planning to relocate more manufacturing stateside, and industry is beginning to reinvest in U.S. plants and equipment. Manufacturers are realigning and rebuilding themselves in order to profitably serve the largest free market in the world. Recent trends indicate a long-awaited shift toward understanding the importance of where one builds, and why.

There are many reasons why conditions here are more favorable than in the past. The economics of off-shoring were always based on a set of unquestioned assumptions. For instance, it was assumed that the biggest and most intractable expense item was assembly labor, which could easily be transplanted to foreign shores at great savings. In reality, for many manufacturers that category of labor may represent only 5 percent of product cost, with finished materials consuming roughly 70 percent and overhead another 25 percent.

Piece parts were a visible expense that went to bid and too often tipped the balance in favor of overseas deals. But what remained behind were management overhead, increased travel time and expense, customs fees, and greater outlays for logistics. Poor quality and lagging time to market were the other big negatives hiding within the columns of standard accounting. These factors were not often assessed and attached to the part or assembly of parts under bid.

Today, total cost of ownership (TCO) is reasserting itself to provide insight into the influence that departments have in creating or cutting costs. It is a key tool for measuring the causality within interdependent operations and generating shareholder profits.

Some U.S. companies are already doing this, but going forward the secret is to harness TCO alongside product simplification and the science of early costing. Product simplification spawns innovation, quality, and cost reduction by guiding engineering teams to combine separate, inefficient parts and functions into elegant, unified structures that do more for less.

A 2013 study by Boston Consulting Group showed increasing interest by many leading U.S. companies to re-shore their production back to the United States from China. China's once cheap labor advantage has turned to an imminent shortage of workers demanding higher wages. This trend to re-shore to the United States is driven by product quality, wages, and closer proximity to customers.

Big challenges remain. Most component suppliers for tech companies are still based in Asia, and China outpaces the United States in the number of skilled engineers required to fill the increasing demand for smart phones and other new devices. But as always, for the small and medium-sized manufacturer, these are simply the facts of life—they are not excuses.

PROFILE: ICESTONE

Challenges to manufacturers come in all shapes and sizes, and not just from China or Washington, DC. They can appear when you least expect them. The only thing that matters is how you and your team respond.

In 2012 Hurricane Sandy blasted up the East Coast, leaving a trail of flooding and destruction. Among the thousands of businesses affected, one Brooklyn-based manufacturer was hit especially hard. Once the storm had passed, IceStone's 38 employees hoped they'd be able to get back to making tables and countertops out of the company's special material of recycled glass and cement. What they found was that the factory's new garage door, which cost $21,000, had been peeled back like the lid of a tin can. On the shop floor, the 70 motors and 5,000 electrical components that made up their factory had been submerged in five feet of water.

There was $6 million of equipment that was intricately connected to all these different pieces and electronic transfers. This was nothing like when you drop your iPhone in a toilet and you can go buy another one. They had no flood insurance. Dal LaMagna, CEO, thought it was game over.

The employees assured him, "No, no, no, we can fix this. We'll take apart every motor, we'll dry everything out, we'll replace the corroded stuff. We can fix this. We don't have to replace the equipment."

Dal told me, "I went and got a Small Business Administration loan. That's another story, but I'm very pro-SBA by the way. I'm anti-bureaucracy, pro-SBA."

IceStone's key to survival was their corporate culture of "responsible capitalism" where the workers are viewed as more vital than the products or services produced by the business.

This corporate culture was deeply ingrained long before Hurricane Sandy hit, and the storm was not the company's first brush with disaster. The company was barely alive when LaMagna joined in 2004. He was not in need of a job. He was actually retired after making his fortune from the sale of Tweezerman, which he founded, the largest manufacturer of tweezers in the world.

LaMagna began investing in companies that were socially and environmentally conscious. The glass recycled by IceStone would normally be dumped in landfills. Instead, their finished "green" products are beautiful tables and countertops that have absolutely no toxins. LaMagna saw an opportunity to help IceStone turn around.

"I took over the company because it was losing money," he told me. "It never made money. It had gone through twenty million dollars and a lot of it was bad luck. What happened is the founders acquired an existing manufacturing facility that they thought was operational, then found out that they had nothing and had to rebuild the whole factory."

To get the company on the right track, LaMagna talked to the investors, who agreed that they were going to empower the employees specifically by giving them 10 percent of the company. He also raised the salaries of the lowest paid employees. He privately sat down with the people who were making under $15 an hour and told them that the company was doing an "adjustment" and raising them to $15. He did not call it a raise; it was a "living wage adjustment."

"That astounded that group," LaMagna said. "It calmed everybody down. They all thought I was going to come in and just cut everything."

"I remember one of my employees, Manny, who was interviewed by the *Daily News*. They said, 'Oh wow, you must be all excited that you now own a piece of the company and you're going to make a lot more money.' Manny replied, 'You know, we're losing money. I don't see how I'm going to make a lot more money, but I'll tell you one thing, I feel very differently about what I do now. When people ask me what I do, I used to say I operated a forklift truck, and now I say I'm a partner in IceStone.' "

Like Henry Ford before him, LaMagna and the investors believe that a better worker is a well-paid one.

LaMagna involved the factory workers in decision-making and management of the company and held classes to teach them about running a company and how to read financial statements. A representative was elected from the shop floor to assume the role as the third managing partner monitoring decision-making.

By 2012 the company had survived the Great Recession and was almost breaking even instead of formerly losing $250,000 a month. Then the hurricane hit. For LaMagna and his employees, saving the company became a personal mission.

And now that the company is in a growth mode, it faces yet another challenge: How to maintain the healthy company culture as employees are added and the organization becomes more complex.

LaMagna knows scaling up while workers continue to be a vital role in company management is absolutely possible. The key is to make employee empowerment part of the company's culture, and to emphasize that everyone is expected to play a leadership role. The CEO needs to emphasize teamwork, be close to and understand the needs of his or her employees.

LaMagna has his sights set on the long view, and his investment in IceStone is very personal. "I'm not the guy who's running around as the entrepreneur making all the decisions and then telling people what to do," LaMagna told me. "I let them do it. However, I do reserve the executive decision. I say that I'm going to make an executive decision even though you guys all disagree with me, and they respect that."

While making money is critical to any business, it cannot be the only metric. "If you're only measuring how much money you can make out of something, you're a sick puppy," he told me. "When you empower your employees, you have a better life. You don't have to worry about things. You don't get the call on a Saturday night saying the factory alarm went off. Somebody else gets it and goes to it. The whole thing is run by the employees. All you do is hold the culture."

That's the leader's number one job: to set the culture. No one else can do it.

THE REGIONALIZATION OF MANUFACTURING

A 2015 study from the University of Tennessee (UT) on outsourcing and global supply chains found that manufacturing capacity is indeed shifting away from China and other parts of Asia. What's happening now, however, is anything but a return to the habits of the past. According to the UT study, companies are adopting a regional model of manufacturing worldwide, not just in the United States. Many companies are shifting to a regional focus for manufacturing and distribution. No more of the old one-size-fits-all approach, predicated entirely on the cost of factory labor.

Regionalization is on the rise, driven in part by the rising cost of manufacturing offshore. In China alone, the price of labor has experienced double-digit increases over the past 10 years. While certain products or commodities will continue to be sourced centrally in areas of lowest-cost labor, the making of higher-valued goods will be distributed widely, in line with targeted areas of demand.

Why the move now? Companies are becoming more sophisticated in their approach to network design. They are adopting better cost models that refute "knee-jerk decisions over *twenty* years of experience." They are uncovering significant areas of expense that they missed the first time around, including transportation, regulatory compliance, and currency exchange.

Supply-chain risk is becoming a major worry. In recent years, businesses have been hit hard by a series of natural disasters and political upheavals. At the same time, the price of fuel has become volatile, forcing a periodic recalculation of key supply-chain costs. Taken together, these factors make the need for good risk management much more important than it was 20 years ago.

Which companies will benefit from regionalization depends on a handful of key characteristics of their products and supply networks. If the cost of goods sold is relatively low compared with logistics cost, then a company might want to reconsider manufacturing in a far-off developing nation. Also a factor is the degree to which sales volumes are distributed around the world; if you sell cars in China, it makes sense to assemble them there, just like Volkswagen assembles cars in the United States.

The study revealed some relocation of manufacturing back to the United States. Our neighbor Mexico and countries in Latin America, which offer a combination of lower labor costs and proximity to major consumer markets, probably stand to gain from the shift away from Asia. Panama, in particular, stands to benefit from the assembly of subcomponents made in Asia, if it can realize certain improvements in its own infrastructure to help it meet the five conditions outlined in Chapter One—free and stable markets, plentiful raw materials, good labor, accessible energy, and leadership.

Regardless of trends or external threats or all that stuff they talk about in grad school programs, every CEO knows one thing: Either you get the job done or you don't. To succeed takes a special combination of dedication, willpower, street smarts, and imagination. But most important, it takes what I call a culture by design, not default. This special combination has to saturate every corner of your company, from the corner office to the mailroom.

How do you develop it? In the following chapters I'll reveal that to develop a culture of your own design, you need The 7 Values of Ingenuity™.

Incorporating The 7 Values of Ingenuity™ is a long-term process. It isn't something that is done in a day by management proclamation. It involves significant cost and organizational effort. The individual

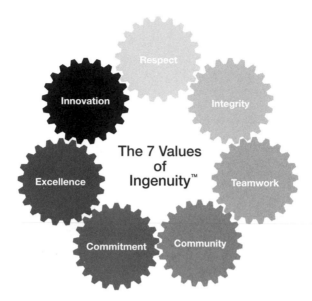

7 Values of Ingenuity™ build upon each other, and each value is dependent on every other value to be effective.

If you are ready to take your organization to the next level and make The 7 Values of Ingenuity™ a vital part of your daily operations and the fabric of your company, then turn the page and read on.

THREE

The 7 Values of Ingenuity™

Most hard-core business executives want new marketing plans, faster machines, and more productive factories. So do I. But consider this: Your competition can buy the same machines as you. They can gin up a new marketing campaign to trump yours, and it is really not that difficult to create a more productive factory. Anyone can do it, and you can bet your competition is planning that right now.

So how do you create a sustainable advantage? With *values*.

But not just any values. You need the right values that move the organization forward, rather than dragging it backward, as too many organization value-sets do.

How do you find the right values and put them to work for you?

One way is to do it the hard way, by trial and error. This is how I did it with my companies. Believe me, over the past 40 years I have made every mistake in the book! Every leader makes mistakes. They are a fact of life.

Sometimes, a big mistake can sink an entire company. Remember Blockbuster Video? Blockbuster was at its peak in 2004, with over 9,000 stores and almost 60,000 employees. A visit to your local Blockbuster store was a regular part of your weekend plans. In 2000, a new upstart video streaming service named Netflix offered to run an online service for Blockbuster to eliminate the cost and time of mailing DVDs.

Blockbuster said no.

You know the story—Blockbuster went bankrupt and Netflix went on to become a huge provider and producer of video content. For Blockbuster, it was a classic case of being fat, dumb, and happy. They were overtaken by a business that at first they had ignored.

Hopefully, the mistakes you make are not as costly as the one made by Blockbuster, and you can pick up the pieces and move forward.

The other way to discover the values that work for a company is to do what you are doing now: by reading this book and learning from my experience. It will save you from having to make every mistake the way I did, and get your business focused on success more quickly.

But I have a word of warning: Reading this book, or any book, is not enough. Please do not think that by reading a book and then putting it back on the shelf that you have accomplished anything. You need to take *action* and discover for yourself how the values I have discovered can work for your organization. They may not work for you in exactly the same way as they work for someone else. You are going to have to experiment and adapt them to your own situation.

Having learned that having a set of bedrock values provides the foundation for sustained success, the question becomes, which values do we adopt? And how do we formulate them?

In my experience, I've been able to boil down the vast number of choices and approaches to the most powerful seven. I call them The 7 Values of Ingenuity™.

Why do I choose the word *ingenuity*?

Because it is the one word that best sums up the common element present in each one of the seven values.

"Ingenuity" is the art of applying inventiveness and originality to conquer challenges. It implies the solving of practical problems; in fact, the Latin *ingenium* is the root word for "engineering." We are talking about building bridges, flying to the Moon, inventing microcircuits—the whole range of our continued efforts to make stuff that helps us live better lives. Ingenuity in humans requires intricate thought processes that combine thoughts and actions, on an individual basis or collectively, to enjoy opportunities and solve problems.

No matter what business you are in, but especially if you are in the business of manufacturing, ingenuity, in all of its many forms, is the one personal characteristic you and every member of your team absolutely must have.

I guarantee you that if you possess the characteristic of ingenuity, you will love your work. It will be a self-reinforcing cycle that will lift you and your company higher. The more ingenuity you have, the more you will love your work; the more you love your work, the more success you will have; and the more success you have, the increased number of opportunities you will have to express your ingenuity. A good example of this is the astonishing career of Thomas Edison. His ingenuity and love of his work took him from his very first patent for an electrographic voice recorder in 1869 to a vast industrial empire encompassing electric light and power utilities, sound recording, motion pictures, and much more.

The 7 Values of Ingenuity™ is not a cookie-cutter or one-size-fits-all solution. Even if your product is similar to something made by others, every company is unique. You and your team are a unique group of people assembled in a particular place for a particular reason. Your company reflects your local standards and customs, and is an expression of the combined efforts of your stakeholders. Therefore, when you adopt The 7 Values of Ingenuity™, their expression will be unique to your organization. They will help you to strengthen your corporate identity and stand out from the crowd.

Your competition can copy your product and duplicate your marketing campaigns. (For example, fast-food industry experts have long commented on the fact that the industry's number two player, Burger King, has a long record of blatantly mimicking the menu offerings of its bigger rival McDonald's.) The only thing your competition *cannot* duplicate is your unique company culture that is based upon The 7 Values of Ingenuity™. It is virtually impossible to copy a culture.

An advantage you have is the fact that most of your competitors will not even try. Or if they try, they will do it half-heartedly and give up before they can go the distance. The 7 Values of Ingenuity™ will give you a competitive edge that is nearly impossible to beat.

The 7 Values of Ingenuity™ have been tested and proven to work. I developed them through 40 years of trial and error (all right, mostly error). I learned the hard way what works and what doesn't, and I learned these lessons in some of the toughest environments you will ever face. Turnarounds. Huge defeats at the hands of competitors. Foreign investors who bought the company only to slash and burn it. And even in these tougher-than-nails environments, the values produced extraordinary gains. In some businesses I ran, I piecemealed one or two of the values, but not all of them. And while even piecemealing some values met with success, it took me nearly 40 years to perfect the formula.

I know what works and what doesn't. I know where the minefields are, and I am painfully aware of the dangers of not eliminating them properly. I know the pain, resistance, and frustration you will face when you start on this journey. It is not an easy one. But if you are persistent and keep ingenuity at the forefront, you will make your company "bulletproof."

Having identified seven key values that form the foundation for success, I am often asked which one is the most important. I understand the question. Picking only one would simplify the matter and make it easier to deal with. People who ask this question usually want to deal with the matter once and be done with it; they want to check it off their to-do list. They liken the issue of values to buying machines or companies. Do it, and then you are done and you do not have to think about it again. They are used to living in the world of black and white. Hard assets. Marketing plans. Capital equipment. Easily understandable and clearly defined.

My answer is always the same: No one value is more important than another. One value doesn't, and can't, live in a vacuum to the exclusion of the others. The synergistic effect of all of the values is what makes them so powerful. As they say, $1 + 1 = 3$. In this case, all seven values create a multiplying effect, much like the compounding effect of money.

The 7 Values of Ingenuity™ are relational, in that each builds upon the other and each value is dependent on every other value to be effective.

For example, some people say *teamwork* is the most important. But how can you expect people to be effective in a team if they are not committed to the mission? How can *commitment* be effective without a drive for *excellence*? And would you really expect people to be able to work effectively in a team if they had no *respect* for each other? *Innovation* cannot live in an organization that is not committed and effective as a team. And there can be no *innovation* if people are not committed to strive for *excellence*. See the point?

Incorporating The 7 Values of Ingenuity™ is a long-term process. It is not something that is done in a day with a management proclamation. It involves significant cost and organizational effort. It is not something that should be undertaken lightly.

Some people see *community* and *integrity* as outliers, and as something I just threw in because they seemed trendy. I didn't. The people who are attracted to a company with community as a core value are seeking a workplace they can call their own and where they can feel a sense of belonging to a community. The principal reason for having that as a core value is that it attracts the kind of employee you want. And when the company supports the local community, the company's employees have a sense of pride in where they work. How many people do you know that do not even want people to know where they work? If you ask them what they do for a living, they give you a vague answer like, "I work in an office" or "I work downtown." They cannot express their ingenuity, and therefore, have little love for their work.

I also believe a company has an obligation to support the community in which its employees earn their living. I am not talking about pure charity, because the business benefits as well. It makes perfect business sense for a company to support, nurture, and develop the social infrastructure from which it draws its current and future employees.

At Miller Ingenuity, we do this in several ways.

First, we take a significant amount of our profit to support local needs.

Second, my employees and I make a significant time commitment to the community.

Let me give you one example. Years ago a flood devastated a town near our headquarters. Not only did we provide money for the relief effort, we gave all of our employees time off with pay to pack food and medical supplies and to man the relief stations. And while this was optional, every single employee participated!

Now maybe you are a gravel-and-guts, "show me the numbers" kind of person who might not see the value in this. But look at it from a purely practical view. In our community, we have no trouble recruiting the best and brightest around, which are the only people that we want. And we do not pay headhunters to find them. Just about everyone in town wants to work for Miller Ingenuity because of our stellar reputation as a community-minded company.

As the company's CEO, I must set the example, and I am happy to do so. I serve on the board of our nonprofit community healthcare system. Between the regular board meetings and committee meetings, I attend 20 meetings a year, all without compensation. Now that is commitment and community all rolled into one!

Integrity is the one value that some people have a hard time relating to. Oh sure, every company has a slogan that says that integrity is important, but you may ask if it can really contribute to the bottom line? And does it really integrate synergistically with the other values?

It does, and here is how.

Suppose you want people to embrace the value of Excellence. But how can there be excellence if people do not have the integrity to own up to a mistake? Or reveal a quality problem they know exists, but might jeopardize the financials if it is exposed?

Integrity is the glue that binds all the values together. Every single employee knows I am as good as my word. If I say something, I will not say it lightly, and they know it can be counted on. My analogy is this: If I need you to jump out of the plane but you are not sure if you can trust me when I said I packed your parachute, are you going to take that leap?

Integrity has to start with the CEO. But it cannot end there. Every single employee has to have it and every single employee has to believe that every other employee has it too. Everyone has to believe that we "have their back." It all starts with integrity.

Is it easy to create and sustain The 7 Values of Ingenuity™? Hardly. It takes years of effort and cost. And it also takes the courage to fire star performers if they cannot or will not live up to the company values. All it takes is one exception to the "golden rules" and people will conclude the rules are not meant for them, or that this values stuff is just a management fad that will soon go away if ignored.

So where do you start? As the CEO, you must first decide to remake the company in the image of these values. Do not take this declaration lightly. It will very likely create much angst and turmoil in the company. And the chances are good that some, if not many, of the people you employ today will not make the trip and will have to be replaced. I speak from experience here. Any time I have created these values in a business I ran, many people had to be replaced because they either did not want to or could not live up to the values. After all, it can be a scary thing for some employees to suddenly be held accountable for teamwork, excellence, and respect (just to name a few), when for years all they have done is walk in the door, punch the clock, go home, and complain to the neighbors what a lousy company they work for.

The worst thing you can do is make a declaration that magically these values are now part of the DNA of the company, just because you say so.

The second-worst thing you can do is pronounce them and then ignore them. Employees will be watching for that; in fact, they will even be expecting it.

THE FOUR PHASES

There is a certain order in which these values should be implemented. In fact, the order is critical, and should be undertaken in four phases.

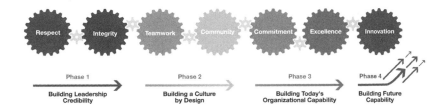

LEADERSHIP CREDIBILITY

The first phase, and the most important, is building *leadership credibility*. This is also one of the most difficult parts of the process. That is because in many organizations, leaders are autocratic and indifferent to their employees. Always remember that you cannot expect people below to be what the top is not. So if the senior leadership team does not possess and demonstrate The 7 Values of Ingenuity™, no one else will. That is why you start at the top.

You will not be starting with a blank slate of leaders. Some will embrace the new values and some won't. You need to remove the ones that won't. It is as simple as that. If you even allow one holdout the entire effort will have no credibility. Remember, values have to trump performance. Do not let your rainmakers act like jerks just because they make rain.

Depending upon the quality of your leadership when you start, the first phase will take one or two years. You will need all this time to replace the leaders you displace and you still need to run the place in the meantime.

Culture by Design

After phase one is in place, then, and *only then*, can you move on to phase two, which is building a *culture by design*. This is where you develop the quality of your workforce and its ability to work as a team. I will take you through that process in Chapters Six and Seven. This process will take another one or two years depending on where you start. Once again, be prepared to make changes in your workforce even if one single employee does not want to be part of the new program.

Building Today's Organizational Capability

Once you have built the culture by design, then you are ready to move on to the next phase, which is building today's organizational capability. For all you hard-nosed businesspeople out there, this is the operational phase. To give you an example of what I mean by operational, this is the phase in which you would implement lean principles into the organization. You would not want to do it before you build the culture because the organization would not be ready for it. In this phase, you can expect to increase efficiency and productivity by orders of magnitude. I know, because I have done it. Do not be tempted to skip to this part, which is in Chapter Nine.

Building Future Organizational Capability

But having a high level of organizational capability will only allow you to deal with today's challenges, not tomorrow's. We cannot know what challenges tomorrow brings, but it is a pretty safe bet they will not be the same as today's. That is what the next phase is for, building future capabilities. This is very difficult because there are no cookie-cutter answers. There are no off-the-shelf programs to guide you through. That is why it is critical that you prepare the organization for a future that is unknown. It will take several years to implement this phase. I will cover that in Chapter Ten.

As you have seen in the previous chapter, I will also include case studies of companies that have overcome tremendous odds to succeed by design. Their stories are inspirational and will help guide you on your journey.

THE 7 VALUES OF INGENUITY™

As I revealed earlier in this chapter, the key to outdoing, outsmarting, and outlasting the competition, particularly in an industry like industrial manufacturing, is one thing: *ingenuity*. Over the past 40 years, I have taken the basic concept of ingenuity and matched it with 7 bedrock values that are essential for success in business. These 7 Values of Ingenuity™ are the ones I have used to propel many companies into mega-growth, in industries as diverse as industrial automation and publishing. They are:

1. Respect
2. Integrity
3. Teamwork
4. Community
5. Commitment

6. Excellence
7. Innovation

These 7 Values of Ingenuity™ need to become part of your company's DNA. Each of these needs to be much more than buzzwords; they should be expectations, cultural metrics, and commandments. They must be infused in everything you do: pay, bonuses, hiring, recruiting, the length of the workweek, inventory management, product development, how you communicate, and the physical environment of the plant itself. All your employees have to own their work. And every single employee has to have a single focus: to make profits.

Profile: J.W. Hulme Co.

The Great Recession hit many American manufacturers hard, especially after commercial credit vanished. During the boom years, when credit had been readily available, principals Chuck Bidwell and Jennifer Guarino of upscale luggage maker J.W. Hulme Co. of St. Paul, Minnesota, had borrowed aggressively. But the recession reduced credit limits, leaving the company with inadequate funds to pay suppliers. Catalogs, which at the time were the focus of Hulme's traditional sales strategy, had to be printed behind schedule.

As the credit crunch squeezed the company, the two owners rose to the challenge and made personal sacrifices to meet expenses, with Guarino contributing cash out of pocket and Bidwell selling his collection of classic cars.

Eventually, Olympus Capital Investments LLC in Morristown, New Jersey, put up a lifesaving 49 percent stake in the company.

The company, which had been established in 1905, stayed in business by knowing when to innovate and when to keep its tried-and-true solutions. The first order of business was to make a sweeping change in the company's outdated technology infrastructure. With help from Olympus, the company introduced an automated ordering system and updated its website. Olympus also urged the company to consider contemporary product designs to augment its traditional line of leather and canvas luggage—for example, a leather case for Apple's iPad, and products in a variety of new colors, departing from its staid brown-leather look.

In a departure from its traditional catalog mail-order sales, Hulme's wares were introduced to Barneys retail stores. The company also pursued

Hollywood movie product placement, including *Rabbit Hole* with Nicole Kidman (it helped that Olympus's sister company, Olympus Productions, produced the film).

When it came to bedrock principles, Hulme found a like-minded partner in Olympus. Other investors who approached the company had suggested wholesale changes, such as departing from the company's "Made in America" brand. More than one equity firm told the company to send their manufacturing to China. But Olympus had an appreciation for the company's legacy. "Made in America" is a key part of the company's identity. Their website says it best:

> For more than a century, every J.W. Hulme Co. travel bag, briefcase, backpack, handbag and accessory has been proudly Made in America and crafted to last a lifetime.

It is all about adding value.

The principals were intent on turning around the company, but not at the expense of the core of what they did. They succeeded in making Manufacturing 2.0 a success by doubling down on quality, dedication, and commitment to excellence in everything they did.

In the next chapter, I will reveal the first of The 7 Values of Ingenuity™, which is *Respect*. It is the foundation for everything that follows, and once you have created a culture of respect, you can begin to take your company higher.

FOUR

The First Value of Ingenuity—Respect

Everyone knows the words of the classic song by the Queen of Soul, Aretha Franklin: "R-E-S-P-E-C-T! Find out what it means to me!"

She is right.

Respect means a lot.

In fact, it is the foundation of The 7 Values of Ingenuity™. And just like the foundation is the first thing you create when you build a house, a foundation of respect is the first thing you create when you build The 7 Values of Ingenuity™.

What is respect?

The dictionary says that respect is "a feeling of admiring someone or something that is good, valuable, or important; a feeling or understanding that someone or something is important and serious, and should be treated in an appropriate way; the polite attitude shown toward someone or something that you consider important." It is the recognition that something or someone deserves to be treated with dignity and in a way that you would want to be treated.

Having respect does not mean that you have to *agree* with everything another person does. Respect has nothing to do with agreement. In fact, respect is often revealed most vividly in those instances when you *disagree* with someone. It is then that your true regard for the other person as a human being is revealed—to yourself, to the other person, and to other people in the company.

Respect is an essential ingredient in a winning company. It is every bit as important as anything else in the business. You can have the best machines, the best marketing plans, and the best strategy, but if you do not have respect, you might as well shut all those machines down and go home.

I have worked for many people who did not respect me or anyone else. It showed in the way they talked to me and the way they treated me. It is not hard to figure out if the guy you work for either respects you as a person and respects your opinions, or disrespects you.

People naturally seek respect. They seek it from their spouses. They seek it from their neighbors. They seek it from the social groups they join. Why do you think so many people join bowling leagues? And why are your employees more interested in their bowling league than they are in your company? They *pay* to bowl. They may not even be that good at it; most people are not. Meanwhile, *you pay them* to work. They are probably good at their work or they would not have a job. Why do they rush off to the bowling alley but drag their butts into work? Maybe because they like to bowl, but I believe bowling leagues meet another need that most work places do not—the need to be respected.

And is your hairdresser really that good, or does she make you feel good by taking an interest in your life and treating you with respect?

Why do you think the fictional characters in *Cheers* hung out at that bar all the time? Because they were treated with respect (well, for the most part) by their friends.

Do your employees find respect everywhere they go except at your company? Then you need to make some changes. Fast.

Respect is a fundamental human need. Abraham Maslow is an American psychologist best known for creating "Maslow's Hierarchy of Needs." It is usually illustrated as a five-layered pyramid, with the largest, basic needs at the bottom and highest needs at the top.

Named as "deficiency needs" or "d-needs" by Maslow, the first four layers beginning from the bottom are: physical needs, security, friendship and love, and esteem. An individual will feel nervous and stressed if these basic needs are not met. According to Maslow's theory, before a person can be focused or motivated on the needs at a higher level, the most basic needs must be satisfied first.

In Maslow's hierarchy, respect is above satisfying basic physical needs. It is an integral part of self-esteem. And what happens when the human need for self-esteem is not met? Well, the answer to that is quite complicated. But put most simply, when self-esteem needs are not met, your employees feel weak, inferior, and incompetent. Does that sound like the formula for highly productive employees to you?

Even worse is when they turn somewhere else to have that need met. To bowling leagues. To lawyers. To labor unions.

You see, your company is already satisfying the lower human needs in Maslow's hierarchy. The wages you pay and the working conditions you provide probably are enough to take care of your peoples' physical needs. In fact, these lower needs of wages and benefits can be viewed by employees as entitlements. Wages and benefits can never satisfy the higher needs. They are never "satisfiers." They can only be "dis-satisfiers" if they are viewed as inadequate. And guess what? Dis-satisfiers are *always* viewed as inadequate. Oh, they may be adequate when you first raise wages, but that only lasts a short time.

A LEADER'S RESPONSIBILITY

As a leader, it is your job to create an environment of respect. The 7 Values of Ingenuity™ start with you, and the first value is Respect.

Do you need grand gestures? Not necessarily. Sometimes the simplest of respectful acts can greatly affect morale, and therefore, productivity. In a company I once took over, I noticed some of our employees were parking their cars in the street. I thought that was odd, so I decided to look into it. It was during the winter and the parking lot along the side of the building was on a slight slope downward toward the street.

The parking area was never paved and was only dirt. Because of the foundation of dirt, in the icy winter, employees' cars would slide into the street. Every so often the employees would go out and pull their cars back into the parking lot.

Apparently, the previous CEO did not think employees were worth the minor expense of paving the lot so their cars would be secure. Needless to say, as soon as I determined the problem, I promptly had the lot paved.

It is a small thing, but it made a difference. It showed the employees that they were respected.

Why should you do these kinds of things? Because your competition can pay the same wages and benefits as you do. Your competition has the same dis-satisfiers as you do. You can never win the dis-satisfier game. Do not even try.

But you can win the respect game. Respect is the foundation for business excellence. Without respect, no business can excel. The reason many businesses languish in low margins and poor profitability is because they have cultures of disrespect and that destroys more businesses than recessions.

RESPECT YOUR CUSTOMERS

If you have a culture of disrespect, your employees probably do not respect the customer, either. Your sales team probably does, but what about all the other touch points your customer has with your company? Cultures of disrespect ooze out of every pore in the company. At every point in the business cycle, from order taking to packing and shipping, disrespect for the customer will be evident everywhere.

Have you ever walked into a restaurant only to be treated disrespectfully by the hostess? Of course you have. It is clear on the first encounter she could care less about you. You can be sure she does not respect her coworkers either. Now, just like sales people, the waiter will show you a great deal of respect, because he wants a tip. But the damage is already done. I know when I have been treated disrespectfully by the hostess, I do not care how nice the waiter is; I will not go back to that restaurant again. And in case you did not know, the lifetime value of a restaurant customer is around $100,000. But what the owner of that restaurant, who just lost one customer forever does not know is this: How many other customers did that hostess treat disrespectfully that day? How many that month? How many that year? You get the point.

But it gets worse.

The same thing happens in your business. Often, it only takes one touch point of disrespect to lose a customer forever. And if your company has a culture of disrespect, your customers are getting bombarded with what I call "disrespectful touch points." Now, you can get away with that if you are DirecTV or DISH Network, because people only have two choices: bad and worse. And airlines are notorious for disrespecting their customers. That is what years of government subsidies will do to you.

But if you are in a competitive field where customers have lots of options, you cannot afford to have a culture of disrespect.

Always appreciate your customers' patronage. When you make a sale, it is certain that your product rather than your competitor's was preferred by your customer based on the quality of your product and reputation of your company. Your gratitude should be relayed to that customer simply by saying "thank you" or in another heartfelt way. Then, follow up at a point in the future to inquire whether the customer is still satisfied—and if not, then find out why.

Value the relationship you have with your customers. Most customers like to do business with people they know. It is easier and more convenient, and the customer knows what to expect. While some customers drift away for reasons you may never know, most customers want the relationship to continue, and they know it needs to be mutually beneficial.

Be respectful of your customer by staying in touch but not being pushy. A constant barrage of sales pitches will create an uncomfortable one-way feeling. Find ways to remind the customer of your interest without constantly flooding them with sales materials. A free newsletter can be a pleasant way to combine useful tips for the customer combined with recent material about your company's products or services.

Care about your customers' concerns. If you can provide ideas or suggestions that can help them do their job more easily or be more successful, it reflects your genuine concern. Positioning your business or yourself as a valuable resource will keep you top of mind with your customers.

For example, at Miller Ingenuity, when our self-directed factory teams are faced with a challenge or motivated by a new solution, they accept full responsibility to meet customers' needs—large and small—in the most inventive and efficient ways possible.

From the team's early morning "Toolbox" meeting where they organize their tasks for the day, to brainstorming, or to producing the highest quality parts, our teams are driven to solving our customers' problems and improving our own internal processes along the way.

> Our sales relationship team, product development engineers, and the operations people support our factory team by walking our customers' shop floors. It's there, where wrenches are turned, that we observe, question, and discover how we can help fix a customer's problem, find a better solution than currently available, or re-engineer and improve an older part. (http://www.milleringenuity.com/capabilities)

Remember what I said about respect playing an important part when you and a colleague do not agree on something? The same goes for your customers. Treating nice, friendly customers with respect is fairly easy. The true test of your character comes when your customer is angry or rude. This is the time that you have to pay particular care to be respectful. The fact is, an irate or upset customer who comes to you is most likely not upset with you personally. He or she is upset about something else that has happened to him or her, and the customer has chosen you to tell about it. For you, his or her unhappiness represents a tremendous *opportunity*.

Be a patient listener and be sure you fully understand his or her problem before you respond to him or her. Do not respond from a script. And if you cannot solve his or her problem, find someone who can.

Keeping your cool and focusing on respecting that unhappy person will bring you personal satisfaction and impress your colleagues; and even if you cannot immediately resolve your customer's issue, you may turn him or her into a loyal customer.

RESPECT THOSE WHO REPORT TO YOU

I once worked for a guy who usually would not acknowledge whether an opinion I put forth was usable. I would have to guess what he was thinking, because he often would not tell me.

When I offered an opinion or made a suggestion, he would not say whether he thought the idea was a good one or not. Once I asked him why he would not comment on them, and he said, "If I tell you if it's good or bad, then I have made the decision for you, and I want *you* to make the decision." That was twisted logic to me because a leader is supposed to lead, not leave his team clueless and in the dark. As a leader, you owe it to the people you lead to mentor them and give them sound advice. How else can they develop? Leaving them in the dark on your views breeds only suspicion that you are setting them up for a fall, or intend to blame them if the decision goes wrong.

And when people think that, as I did, it creates only mistrust between the leader and his team. And mistrust could not exist where respect does.

I found his approach not only counterproductive but offensive and disrespectful. And always remember, disrespectful cultures are a breeding ground for poor performance. When leaders make people feel bad about themselves by disrespecting them, how can they perform at their best? When coworkers make each other feel bad with disrespect, how can they possibly function well as a team?

ALLEN-BRADLEY CULTIVATES RESPECT

Nearly 40 years ago, I was fortunate enough to start my leadership career at Allen-Bradley (A-B) based in Milwaukee. With revenues of approximately $6.61 billion as of May 2015, A-B (now a subsidiary of Rockwell Automation) was, and still is, a world-class company that pioneered the industrial automation industry. They manufacture programmable logic controllers (PLC), human-machine interfaces, sensors, safety components and systems, software, drives and drive systems, contactors, motor control centers, and systems made of these and similar products.

They have also pioneered the best practices in leadership in the world.

A-B knew a lot about how to respect people. The founder, Harry Bradley, used to live in an apartment on the top floor of the factory, and he would often visit with employees on the third shift—not to be sure they were working, but to be sure were being treated well. His outlook and people philosophy permeated the entire organization. Leaders at A-B were trained and expected to treat people with dignity and respect.

I once did a stint in the human resources function. The company had a remote manufacturing plant that needed to replace the human resource manager, who had left the company. They needed someone to fill in while they searched for a permanent replacement. I took on the job expecting the assignment would be a piece of cake—a "turn the lights on, turn the lights off" kind of thing until the permanent replacement was found.

It turned out to be anything but a piece of cake. The plant was a swamp of employee discontent and bad management. Headquarters, and my boss, had no idea how bad things were. In fact, when I arrived, the employees were actively seeking out a union to protect them from the managers. Remember what I said about people seeking out unions to gain respect?

To put this in context, most of A-B was union-free and it had a corporate edict to stay that way. It was common knowledge that any human resource guy who let one of his facilities bring in a union would get the boot. That guy would be my boss, so he was very motivated to get it fixed.

Unfortunately, the head guy at the facility—the plant manager—was the problem. He ran the place like a plantation. He treated people badly. He was without a doubt the worst leader I have ever seen. And he was not about to let some snotty-nosed kid from HQ mess up his life, so he did everything he could to give *me* the boot. Remember, A-B prided itself on how it treated its employees, so this situation could have been a major disaster if something was not done about it.

One day I was on the factory floor getting feedback about the problems from one of the employees. I suddenly heard my name paged on the loudspeaker to call the plant manager. Someone told him I was on the floor "stirring things up." And was he ever mad! He asked me, "Are you out there talking to someone about problems?" When I said I was, he said, "You'd better get your ass back in here."

Now that's respectful, isn't it?

I was not about to go back to HQ with my tail between my legs, so I stuck it out, shuttling between employees and reporting back my findings to HQ (since I could not rely on the plant manager to fix problems he created). The next several months were hell because the plant manager treated me worse than he did everybody else.

Then, in a classic A-B move, upper management fired the plant manager. Not because the plant was performing badly (it was performing well), but because he treated people badly.

Thus, early in my career I was immersed in a business culture of caring, respect, compassion, and fairness. I "studied" under the masters. I worked for people who were absolute models of superstar leadership. And I soaked it all in. I never forgot those lessons.

In my world, respect trumps performance every time. I do not care how well one of my leaders is performing. If he treats people badly, I give him the boot. I have done it many times before and I will do it again. So should you.

Why? Because bad people managers will never be able to sustain good performance. When people are treated disrespectfully, one of two things occurs: if they are any good, they leave the company, and then you lose a star performer. If they stay because they think they cannot get another job, they mentally check out because of the way they are treated. Or even worse, they might intentionally perform poorly, just to "get back at the boss."

No, never allow a manager to treat employees disrespectfully, no matter how good the performance. Great performance without respect is always a temporary condition. As a leader, you earn the right today for great performance from your employees as long as you are treating them well. And then you earn the right tomorrow. Always remember the "earn" part. Never feel as though you are "entitled" to a certain level of performance from your team. They owe you nothing. You owe them. Do not ever forget that.

And from a psychological point of view, respect is extremely important. We all need to be respected, to have self-esteem, and self-respect. It is a perfectly normal human desire to be accepted and valued by others. All your employees want to be engaged in activities that give them a sense of contribution. They want to feel accepted and self-valued. Most people seek this in the workplace.

RESPECT CAN BE A SCARCE COMMODITY

Fewer workers feel respected than you might imagine. According to a study of 20,000 employees conducted by Harvard Business School and Tony Schwartz, half of them did not feel respected by their bosses.

So what? What is the big deal?

It is a huge deal. The study says that "being treated with respect was more important to employees than recognition and appreciation, communicating an inspiring vision, providing useful feedback—even opportunities for learning, growth, and development. Those who get respect from their leaders reported 56% better health and well-being, 1.72 times more trust and safety, 89% greater enjoyment and satisfaction with their jobs, 92% greater focus and prioritization, and 1.26 times more meaning and significance. Those who feel respected by their leaders were also 1.1 times more likely to stay with their organizations than those that didn't."

According to the same study, "Respect also had a clear impact on engagement. The more leaders give, the higher the level of employee engagement: People who said leaders treated them with respect were 55% more engaged."

So the big deal is that respect for the individual has a direct correlation to the performance of the organization. As it turns out, "nice" does contribute to profit.

So the upside is that respect results in greater performance. What about the downside? What happens when people do not feel respected by their leaders? According to Abraham Maslow, deprivation of these needs can lead to an inferiority complex, weakness, and helplessness. And psychological imbalances, such as depression can occur. Does not sound like a healthy environment designed to stimulate high performance, does it?

And when people feel weak or helpless in the workplace, they turn to people and organizations that can help them. Like labor unions, lawyers, and the Department of Justice. None of which have the best interests of your business at heart. And always remember this: When employees vote for a union, they are really voting against the company. They are voting against their leaders.

RESPECT MUST BE WOVEN INTO EVERY POSITION IN THE COMPANY

It is clear that leaders must respect their employees if they want high performing organizations. But I also contend that the organization cannot perform at its peak unless respect goes beyond just how the leaders treat their employees. Every person in the company has to be respectful of every other employee. The entire company has to have respect for one another.

I once took over a business that was a cesspool of disrespect. The way people treated each other was horrible. The white-collar employees had their own cafeteria because they did not want to be around the factory employees. Factory employees did not even have a cafeteria and were not allowed to use the white-collar one.

The language that people in the factory used with one another was more like what you might find in a prison than in a business. I am talking about the vilest of four letter words. Sometimes the words would escalate to fights and physical abuse. It was that bad.

One thing I have learned over the years is that respect, or lack of it, is rooted in the language people use with one another—or more to the point, the language that the leaders permit. So the very first thing I did was call the entire company together and declare a zero tolerance policy for foul language.

I explained to everyone the fundamentals of respect and how important it was to treat each other as teammates, not cellmates. And I clearly outlined the consequences of ignoring the new policy: immediate termination. No warnings, no second chances. Out the door—period.

As I expected, the new policy was immediately tested. I fired a guy within hours of the announcement. The next day I fired two more. At this point I was beginning to wonder if I would have any employees left by the end of the week! And amazingly enough, many of the employees felt I had taken away a God-given right to swear!

I stuck to my guns because I knew this was the first and most important battle to win the war for respect. And that if I did not stay the course I had no chance in creating respect as a core value in the company.

And over time, the employees who could not fit into a culture of respect either left or were asked to leave. And those that stayed felt much more valued and enjoyed an atmosphere of camaraderie and fulfillment. Does this sound like pie in the sky? It is not. I have done it and seen the immense benefit to the bottom line.

PROFILE: BILL McDERMOTT AND SAP

One of the most respectful leaders I know is Bill McDermott, the CEO of the German software giant, SAP. SAP serves over 282,000 customers in over 190 countries. With billions in revenue, he oversees an enterprise involving diverse cultures.

Bill was gracious enough to let me interview him for my "League of Extraordinary CEOs" column that appears monthly in the *American City Business Journals* (www.bizjournals.com). I could not believe that a guy running a company that huge would take the time to talk to me.

But within two minutes of our meeting, I knew why. He is the most humble and unassuming guy you will ever meet. One of the things that struck me about him is how much he respects people in his organization —and their opinions.

When he was first elevated to CEO of SAP, it was to colead the company with a co-CEO. He ascended to the sole CEO position in 2014. Do you think they would have given him the sole CEO job if they did not trust him and if he did not respect everyone around him? Hardly.

And even now he coleads the company with the unions that represent the employees, as they have representatives on the board. And he does it in such a respectful manner that it is hard not to see the role respect plays in his leadership and in his success.

In fact, I would say a cornerstone of his leadership success is the respect he has for everyone's opinions. He will tell you that he is "more humble than ever." Clearly humility is an essential ingredient of respect.

And while Bill is a humble man, the antithesis of humility and respect is arrogance. Have you ever known anyone who was arrogant who showed respect?

Bill builds relationships based on a foundation of trust and respect. This formula has propelled his life and career—and it all began with a dream.

In his book *Winners Dream: A Journey from Corner Store to Corner Office*, McDermott relates his career journey and encourages anyone who has a dream to follow it with a strong belief, because it just may come true. (http://www.bizjournals.com/bizjournals/how-to/growth-strategies/2015/01/sap-ceo-mcdermott-describes-career-formula.html?page=all)

Bill would tell you that he has built his whole career upon being as good as his word, and on trust. But how could anyone trust him if he did not show respect for them?

His respect for others not only won him the SAP job but made him extraordinarily successful in it.

HOW TO INSTILL RESPECT

So how do you instill a culture of respect in your organization? How do you make respect a core value?

First, as the leader you have to lead by example. If you are not an inherently respectful person, you do not have a chance. You have to genuinely care about your employees. You have to care about their personal lives, their hopes and dreams, their financial situation, and how they feel about the workplace.

Of course we all have bottom lines to worry about, but I am proof positive that you can care about people and profit at the same time. After all, how can one exist without the other?

So let's assume that you are a respectful person who cares about your people. Here is what you have to do: Declare to your leaders that respect will be a cornerstone value. You need to make sure they all understand the role that respect can play in the success of the company and why it is so important.

You know who the leaders are who do not treat people with respect. It is too late to turn them around. Employees already know they are jerks, and you cannot turn a jerk into a nice guy. Once a jerk, always a jerk. Plan on replacing them. Remember, your people are always watching you and they will assume this is just another management fad until you prove otherwise. When you take out the jerks, they will applaud you.

Make a huge part of the managerial incentive program contingent on demonstrating the value of respect. Make it a formal part of your performance appraisal process.

Declare to the entire company that respect will be a core value. Make sure all the employees understand what respect means; do not just use the term *respect*. Talk about thoughtfulness, caring for each other, and so forth.

Make respect a formal part of the rank and file employee appraisal process. You will not have to do this forever, but you will have to do it for a while so people know you are serious about it.

Put a stake in the ground that extreme disrespect is an offense that will result in termination. Otherwise, it is just a management platitude. And then be prepared to terminate people—even star performers who violate that rule. In fact, people probably will not believe how serious you are about respect until you do fire someone.

Celebrate people who demonstrate this value at every chance you get. Reward them at every chance you get. Repeat after me!

FIVE

The Second Value of Ingenuity—Integrity

Merriam-Webster defines *integrity*, in part, as "the quality of being honest and fair." Isn't it interesting that "fair" is a part of integrity? Others have defined integrity as "doing the right thing in a reliable way," or "doing the right thing even when no one is looking." And to round out the common definition, there is "steadfast adherence to a strict moral or ethical code, such as a leader with great integrity."

People with integrity are as good as their word. They do what they say, and can be relied upon to do the right thing. But "the right thing" is sometimes in the eye of the beholder. As an example, when I was in graduate school, one of the classes was The Ethical and Legal Environment. It was an interesting class because we examined case studies of business situations to determine if they were both ethical and legal.

Some cases, while they were within the confines of the law, were not necessarily ethical. Conversely, while some cases were ethical, they were not necessarily legal.

A case in point is antitrust law. Antitrust law does not necessarily concern itself with the ethics of a market situation. Many antitrust laws arose not from ethical considerations, but from concerns about market allocation and concentration of market power. Thus, according to these antitrust laws, many perfectly ethical situations could very well be illegal.

Most people would agree that someone with high ethics has integrity. And most people would agree that a person with integrity must have high standards of ethics. Or would they? Those classes heightened my awareness on the subject of ethics and integrity. Integrity is not necessarily an absolute that can be clearly defined and agreed upon by all in every situation as a universal truth. Much like ethics and the law, integrity is more situational than absolute.

Without having a scientific test for integrity, you need to rely upon your common sense and personal morality. In 1964, in writing his opinion in an obscenity case, United States Supreme Court Justice Potter Stewart famously said, "I know it when I see it." When it comes to matters of integrity, most people "know it when they see it." And they are looking for it all around them. They are hoping to see it in their government. They are hoping to see it in their school districts. They certainly hope to see it with their healthcare providers.

But what does integrity mean in an organizational setting? And why does it play such an important role in revitalizing American manufacturing in general? And why should it be a foundational principle in your organization specifically? These are the questions we will answer in this chapter.

LESSONS FROM REAL LIFE

I once owned a classic cherry-red 1968 Mustang convertible. Oh, how I loved that car! It did not have a scratch on it. And I was the proverbial "little old lady who only drove it to church on Sundays." The first winter I had it, I needed to find a place to store it, as my garage was not big enough. So I got the idea to store it in the company warehouse. I could do that, right? After all, I was the CEO and we had plenty of space to park the car.

The day I was to bring it in, I was walking through our factory and could not help but notice one of the values banners we have hanging from the ceiling. And that is when it hit me like a lightning bolt. The value banner of Integrity jumped right out at me. And it got me thinking. Even though I was the CEO, and even though the warehouse had the space to store the Mustang, was it the right thing to do? I could not help but ask myself, would a leader with integrity store his personal car in the company warehouse? The answer screamed out at me: "Absolutely not!"

So I never did store my car there. But what if I had? Would it have made a difference as far as my employees were concerned? You bet it would. Your people are always watching you. They are always taking cues from how you behave. You cannot preach integrity and not practice it. In fact, if you preach any value, you'd better practice it yourself.

Had I stored my car there, people would have scratched their heads, wondering if this whole integrity thing was just a slogan or a real value that they should live by. How could I have expected them to have integrity if I did not demonstrate it? If I had stored my car there, the whole value of integrity would have gone up in smoke.

But why is it so important for everyone in an organization to have integrity? Because at its most fundamental level, integrity is the glue that binds the organization together. People can perform at a high level only if they believe in their teammates. They have to know when they jump out of that airplane that their teammate packed the parachute properly. They have to believe when their teammate tells them something, that it is the gospel truth. Otherwise they will always hold back, wondering if the information they received is reliable or not.

I once hired an executive who had spent years working for another company where integrity was not high on their list. In fact, I do not think it was on their list at all. Apparently, this executive had been burned by bosses who would authorize him to do something; but if it turned out badly, they would deny they ever gave him the authorization. Now that is lack of integrity. How could this executive ever confidently march into the battle if he believed the general would abandon him at the slightest hint of trouble?

Many times, I would give him the go-ahead to do a task or project, only to have him come back to me a few days later and ask me if I was *really sure* that was what I wanted him to do.

Unfortunately, this story does not have a happy ending. This executive had been so conditioned to working in an integrity-free zone full of backtracking and backstabbing that he could not bring a project or a task to completion. He kept dithering and hemming and hawing.

I am a compassionate person. I believe in giving everyone a fair chance. And when I say I am going to give you a chance to prove yourself, I will give you a chance. But in business the stakes are very high, and I cannot afford to jeopardize everyone else's job because one person cannot get his or her act together. To coddle one employee is not fair to all the others who are working their tails off. Yes, this is another facet of integrity. A leader cannot bend the rules or relax the standards for one person. It would have been like allowing this executive to park his car in the warehouse. The message it would have sent to the company would have been terrible.

I had to ask this executive to leave the company because he had no integrity. Not that he was a bad guy, or a dishonest guy. He had no integrity because he agreed to go out and do something, but then he did not. That is a lack of integrity.

I once had another executive who lost integrity that he once had. We were in a competitive bidding situation and we had a disagreement as to where we should go on price. He felt very strongly that I was wrong and he felt he knew better.

He agreed to the price that I wanted. He told me this, to my face. But even though he agreed to go into the bidding process with a certain price, when he made his bid, he quoted the price that he had favored and that I had rejected.

When I found out, I was furious. As I have always said to my team, the time for debate is *before* we run the play. After we come out of the huddle I expect you to run the play I called. After that incident, in my eyes he lost all integrity. I could never again rely on him. And remember, an essential ingredient of integrity is reliability. I had no choice but to let him go.

Another time a manufacturing employee was "fudging" his production numbers. It was not a big fudge, just a series of little fudges. They were so small that you could not even call them falsifications. But let's face it: Little fudges start adding up to big fudges. And if everyone in the whole place thinks little fudges are okay, imagine the mess you would be in at the end of the month. That employee did not think anyone was looking. Remember, integrity is doing the right thing even when no one is looking. In fact, it is essential to believe your people are doing the right thing all the time because it is virtually impossible to be looking all the time. If your people have integrity, you do not have to constantly look over their shoulders.

What did we do about the fudging employee? What we had to do: We fired him because he lost integrity.

Dismissing that employee sent a very clear message to everyone else as to the importance of integrity. If we had simply overlooked it, we would be sending the wrong message. We would have been sending the message that "a little fudging is okay." We would have been sending a message that integrity is not really that important.

We would have been sending the message that parking your car in the warehouse was okay because, hey, it is just a little thing that no one will notice. But if you have a high-performing team, then everyone notices everything.

They notice if projects are not completed on time.

They notice if the price is not what it was supposed to be.

They notice if the numbers do not quite add up correctly.

And guess what: Your customer notices these things too.

Your customer sees that the delivery is late.

Your customer sees a discrepancy in the pricing, or mysterious "hidden charges."

Your customer sees slight variations in the product specs.

If we had not taken action to preserve the integrity of our workplace, we would have been on our way to becoming what I call an "integrity-free" company.

Just imagine a whole company of integrity-free people.

No one would trust anyone else. No one could be counted on to do what they say. No one would believe what anyone says. Everyone would second-guess everyone else. No one would make a move because they would not know if the other guy meant what he said.

In "integrity-free" companies, no one has your back. In fact, everyone will stab you in the back to save themselves.

Can you imagine how poorly companies like this perform? Actually, you do not need to imagine it. Just read a case study of General Motors (GM) during the period from the 1980s to its bankruptcy in June 2009. The story of GM during its 30 years of decline is the story of a total and massive loss of integrity. Executive coddling, union greed, shoddy manufacturing, lack of ingenuity—it is a textbook example of how to ruin a great company. Fortunately, GM has risen from the brink of total disaster, and this once proud American manufacturer is regaining its stature as a global industrial leader.

INTEGRITY-RICH COMMUNICATIONS

As a leader, one of the most important things you must do is practice what I call "integrity-rich" communications. It starts with total, unvarnished honesty. Some leaders are afraid to be honest with their employees because they are afraid the employees cannot handle the truth. And others tell half-truths because they are afraid the whole truth might scare them. Or worse yet, might upset them.

So what they do is keep their people in the dark, especially concerning matters that might adversely affect them, such as deteriorating business conditions that might cause layoffs. That is a huge mistake. People sense when things are not going well, and when you do not talk about it they assume the worst, which is usually worse than it really is. And when you are not bone-honest with them all the time, they will not believe anything you tell them any of the time. And if they do not believe anything you tell them any of the time, you can no longer lead them.

Other leaders are more paternalistic and try to protect their people from bad news. I once served on the board of a university that was facing deep budget cuts. These cuts were certain to adversely affect not only the students, but the faculty as well.

We were sitting around the board meeting table talking about the best way to communicate the problem. Most of the board members took the paternalistic approach. They wanted to protect the students and faculty from the situation, and they did not want mass defections if they found out the truth. This kind of thinking is pure folly! "These are adults," I said, "and you should treat them like adults, not like little kids. And besides, do you think they don't know this is coming? If you choose not to reveal everything you know, they will never trust you with the truth again. And once 'trust in truth' is gone, you can never get it back."

I failed to convince my fellow board members of this approach and they chose the approach of "tell half the truth and hope the other half never shows up." It is hard to estimate the credibility the board lost that day. The sad part is that the changes that had to be made were more protracted and painful than they needed to be.

If you went to your doctor and had some tests done, what would you want your doctor to tell you? Would you want him or her to say, "Here is what the tests reveal: You have cancer. It requires treatment. Here's how we're going to attack it. It's going to be difficult and painful, but if we work together, we can beat it." That's the approach that shows integrity.

Or would you want your doctor to say, "Yes, we took some tests, and we know you have a problem, but we're not going to get into the details because we don't want to upset you. However, you need to report to the hospital for surgery."

Isn't it arrogant to think that you can handle bad information, but others cannot? What makes you so special?

So always remember that your employees want you to have the integrity to "trust in the truth." Tell the truth and trust that your people can deal with it. You may very well have to help them deal with it, but deal with it they must.

If you do not tell them the truth, or if they even think you are not, they will start making things up. And I guarantee you that what they make up will be worse than what you can tell them. And while they are kibitzing about a variety of disaster scenarios, how much work do you think is being done?

But, you say, what if the truth actually is really, really bad? Then you have even more reason to be honest.

I once bought a company in Southern California. Our plan was to shut the plant down, lay off all the employees, and consolidate the business in our own facility. Naturally, my operations people were fearful that if the California employees knew of our plan, they would revolt, sabotage everything in sight, and generally make our lives miserable on their way out. Now that is what I call really, really bad.

The people in California knew we had the equipment and capacity to make the products they were making. Any idiot could figure out we would not want a plant thousands of miles away if we could do it ourselves. So what do you think the California people were thinking? Well, my guess is they had our plan all figured out and expected us to lie about it. Or not reveal the whole truth.

Instead, we trusted in the truth.

I had my guys put together a contingency plan for the worst scenario—all the employees walking out and sabotaging the place. And I had my human resource people put together a generous retention bonus if people stayed and cooperated until we transitioned the business to our place.

And then I stood in front of all the California people and told them the ugly truth: Although I regretted the decision, I had no choice but to shut the place down. And guess what? They were astounded that I told them the truth. And when I told them about the retention package, they were very grateful for what we were doing. No sabotage, no mass walkouts, just an orderly transition where we didn't miss a beat.

And speaking of integrity-rich communications, what do you think our home office employees would have thought about us lying about our plan? They would certainly know we lied because they were having regular contact with the California people. You guessed it, the home office people would wonder if they could ever trust us again. They would wonder if this whole integrity thing was just a management fad.

Again, speaking of integrity-rich communications, never miss an opportunity to let your people know the bad things that can happen if the company does not continue to prosper. Whenever I shut down an acquisition and move its operations to the home office, I give the same speech to the home office employees. In a nutshell, it is "There but for the grace of God, go we." I tell people that it is always better to be the acquirer than the company being acquired. This is because the company being acquired often gets shut down and people lose their jobs. And I very frankly and candidly say the way not to become the company that gets acquired and shut down is to get better every day.

These are "teachable moments" that you should take full advantage of.

Now some people would say you should not scare people like that. I say it is not scaring people when you tell them what they have a *right* to know, and what they *should* know. It is just like your doctor who gives you the straight report about your tests.

Now getting bad news might very well scare them, but they should know what can happen to a company that is not growing. If they know the consequences, they will work harder and with more interest than if they think Disneyland will always be open no matter what.

Performance matters. What people do every single day, in every single function, matters. Leaders with integrity always trust in the truth and tell people what they not only need to, but also should know. Just be sure and follow the discussion with, "But that is not going to happen here if we all do such and such." Let them know how they can help shape their futures, and not just be victims of it. If you tell them only the bad things that can happen without giving them hope, inspiration, and the battle plan, they are bound to be scared. That is not a place you want them to be.

Consider the flip side. Let's assume you never told your team "What could happen if," and then one day the "if" came along and you announced a layoff. How would you handle the question, "Why didn't you ever tell us this could happen? If we had known, we might have worked harder, or smarter, or more as a team." That is a question you should never have to answer.

Remember, this is not Sunday school and these are not children. Talk to them like adults, not like idiots who are not smart enough to understand the world around them. The more you talk to them, and the more you talk to them with integrity, the more they will feel enabled and in control. And without question, employees who feel enabled and in control are more productive than those who do not.

When employees do not feel enabled and in control, they spend all their time worrying about the unknown. And they spend all their time trying to find ways to become enabled and in control of things that either are not relevant or may even be destructive.

A dissatisfied warehouse worker will take control of his personal schedule by coming late to work.

An unhappy salesman will take control of his job by quoting his price, not the company's price.

Assembly line workers who feel disrespected will seek respect in the union hall.

An executive who is worried about getting laid off will do the least amount of work possible while surreptitiously looking for another job.

These are all negative consequences stemming from poor leadership decisions not to trust in the truth.

GOOD INTENTIONS, BAD RESULTS

It is not that poor communicators are always bad people. What I see too often are leaders who are just plain bad communicators. They may be good at the technical aspects of their job, but they missed Communication 101 in college.

Sometimes I find leaders who are too scared to tell the truth, like the board members at the university. While as individuals the board members possessed *personal* integrity, they did not understand the concept of *organizational* integrity. While as individuals they would have demanded straight answers from their doctors, they did not understand that as university board members, they themselves were like doctors; their patients included every staff member, teacher, and student at the university. Every individual member of the university community deserved to be treated with *respect* (Ingenuity Value #1) and *integrity* (Ingenuity Value #2).

The last category I see is what I call "King Kong" leaders. They do not feel the need to tell anybody anything. They think that whatever they do is self-evident. They think their employees are mind readers and their customers are sheep. If you are a King Kong leader, you have two choices: get really good at communicating or get out of leadership altogether.

Integrity sounds like a "soft skill," something that is more luxury than necessity. But it is mission critical to tell your people what you are going to do, and then do it.

We all make mistakes, but the only way to display true integrity is by being truthful in words and deed, even if it means apologizing from time to time and fixing what you have broken.

IF IT WERE EASY, EVERYBODY WOULD DO IT

Let's face it: *Integrity* is one of those foolproof words that everybody uses. You see the word in nearly every company's mission statement. Being against integrity is like being against mom and apple pie. And for good reason—integrity must be the fundamental building block to succeed in business. Integrity should be a given, without the need to broadcast its existence.

Yet too many individuals and companies fall short of their stated goal of operating with integrity.

Why is it so difficult for so many companies to attain the clear goal of integrity?

Part of the challenge is what I talked about in the beginning of this chapter. "Integrity" can mean different things to different people. For example, a corporation that seeks to "own" its market may be acting with integrity and still run afoul of antitrust laws.

Humans have a natural characteristic to justify their conduct. College students will agree that it is wrong to cheat. Yet studies confirm many have done so. Why? Because they have found themselves in a situation where they had to make a quick decision. They have to write a term paper or flunk the class. Out of expediency, they buy a term paper. In hindsight, they justify it as "not a big deal" or "everybody does it" and still consider themselves as being honest.

We all face regular integrity-based decisions. Giving feedback at work, filling out business expense forms and billable time sheets, for example. Every contingency cannot be defined in corporate policies.

And, like the student who buys a term paper, sometimes the bad things that we do can seem to be "victimless" crimes. After all, pleads the student, who got hurt when he bought a term paper? Or the worker who says, "Fudging my numbers doesn't hurt anybody else."

This is why, at the end of the day, the company leader must say, "No, you cannot fudge your numbers, not even a little bit. It's just plain wrong and dishonest. I'm not going to get into a philosophical argument with you about it. If you won't provide the exact, real numbers, I'll get someone who will."

Reminders about integrity in statements on corporate values are also about personal responsibility, not just business. As a leader, you need to make sure that if an employee is confused about what constitutes integrity, you will be very happy to tell them in clear, plain English.

PROFILE: COTTAGE GARDEN

Founded in 1996 by Angela Timm, Cottage Garden, Inc. has become America's number one manufacturer and supplier of music and jewelry boxes and sentiment frames. The company had very humble beginnings; it was originally staffed by stay-at-home moms, and they shipped products out of Angela's two-car garage. As the company grew, Angela kept her focus on these principles: a fair price for retailers, fixtures would be free and outstanding service to customers. Her approach worked, and the fledgling company saw its growth double each of the next six years.

In 2000, Angela's husband, Mark, a sales and marketing professional, took over as president to manage the company. Speaking in 2014 to an audience at Ivy Tech Community College in Greencastle as part of the Business and Entrepreneurial Services (BES) Center speakers program, Mark Timm said the story of Cottage Garden's success was steeped in the company's ethics of integrity, hard work, and excellence. "You don't have to have an incredible idea," he told the audience. "You have to be incredible at your idea. That's the story of Cottage Garden. You simply have to be great at your idea."

Timm also said that "doing business great was a big part of the success" of their gift industry venture that started with an idea of supplying retailers rather than running a retail business. By shipping fast and never back-ordering anything, Timm found that retailers readily beat a path to his door.

In 2007, Cottage Garden was named the Indiana Small Administration Business of the Year and finished as the National Small Business of the Year runner-up.

Although his company has evolved into the gift industry's top seller of musical gifts like music boxes, Timm said he learned the award was not based on his bottom line or sales volume. Those state and federal honors, he said organizers told him, were the by-product of "how you do business." And that "how" included not only being great at your gifts and being grateful for your gifts but giving back as well, Timm said. Gratitude does not have to be a big thing; a smile or words of encouragement can "let people know they have value."

"People, purpose, and passion are key ingredients," he said. "Those gifts for which a businessperson should be eternally grateful," he said, "include customers, staff, and co-workers."

The road to success was not without huge challenges. In 2003, Cottage Garden was on the brink of failure. Mark and Angela Timm had maxed-out credit cards and a line of credit they thought they could never repay. Everyone was discouraged, from the owners to the Cottage Garden employees. As if things were not bad enough, the Timms and their company were put to a massive test on a stormy July day. Mark Timm was away on business in Atlanta, and he was talking on the phone to Angela when she mentioned how strange the weather had become, and how it went from windy and threatening to dead calm.

A Midwest farm boy at heart, Timm knew exactly what that meant. He told Angela to immediately go to the basement.

Seconds later an F2 tornado struck the Timm's home west of Bainbridge, Indiana. While fortunately no one was injured, the damage to the house was catastrophic. Wooden beams from a nearby barn shot "through the house like missiles." Debris from the roof rained down upon the interior of the house, with lumber landing on the bed where one of the Timm children had been sleeping.

"The story wasn't the tornado," Mark Timm later said, "but what happened after."

Within 30 minutes of the storm striking the Timm house, the staff of Cottage Garden had arrived at the home. They set about clearing debris, covering exposed areas with tarps, and lending support and manpower wherever necessary or possible.

The same spirit was needed to resurrect the business, which was faltering. Angela and Mark told their employees exactly what was happening, and let their employees know that everyone's help was needed to save the business.

Using teamwork to save the business is exactly what they did.

As Mark told his Ivy Tech audience in 2014, "That set something in motion for Cottage Garden that became the defining moment for our company." It conveyed something Mark believes could not have happened without the people, purpose, and passion elements of the business sense he prescribes.

Can every business disaster be turned around with a combination of a positive attitude and teamwork? Perhaps not—but I will guarantee you that without these values, recovery will be impossible. When business owners stop hiding from their difficulties and communicate with employees, the power of teamwork really kicks in. Suddenly the focus is not on what has happened, or what should have happened, but on what can happen from that point forward. A focus on future action is the most powerful and encouraging turnaround of all!

Cottage Garden, which is now a division of Roman, Inc., is now the largest producer of sentimental music boxes in North America, with more than 600,000 boxes sold each year.

SIX

The Third Value of Ingenuity—Teamwork

One of today's most overused business buzzwords is *team*. Everybody talks about teams. Most business leaders talk about the need for teams and how the organization is just one big happy team. Few would deny that teamwork is the most effective way to optimize results.

But if every organization were just one big happy team, why are so many organizations dysfunctional? If teamwork is the way to go, why don't many businesses have effective teams, even if they say they want to?

As I have said before in this book, if it is so great, why is everybody not doing it?

They are not doing it because it is *difficult*. Building and maintaining a championship team—whether you are manufacturing widgets or trying to win the Super Bowl—is not an easy task. It takes effort and self-sacrifice. It is not a job for the fat, dumb, happy CEO who does not want to get down into the trenches with his or her employees.

And it is absolutely not a job for a leader who has not yet mastered the first two of my 7 Values of Ingenuity™: Respect and Integrity. If you have not yet instilled those values in your organization, I suggest you go back and do it. You need a strong foundation before you can build your skyscraper.

THE MEANING OF TEAMWORK

On those occasions when I have taken over a poorly performing organization, one of the biggest problems I have found is that while everyone talked about teamwork, few people knew what it meant. They did not know what a good team looked like, much less how to create one. Most organizations I have seen tell their people they want teamwork, and then let it go at that. They simply make the declaration and expect it to take shape on its own. They expect—and hope—that once the declaration is made, people will "work together." And what does "work together" mean anyway? Does it mean to agree on everything? Does it mean to share resources? Does it mean to avoid conflict? Most organizations do not even define what teamwork looks like. No wonder employees are confused.

And another obstacle to teamwork is that most organizations have internal processes and policies that actually drive people to *work apart*, not together.

Let me give you just a few examples.

Most employee performance appraisals are done for an individual, not the team to which he or she is a part. But how can you expect an individual to put the team first when he is critiqued only on his own individual performance?

The same thing applies to individual departments. Quality has its goals. Manufacturing has its goals. Marketing has it goals. And they are very seldom, if ever, in alignment with each other. How can you expect Marketing to work as a team with Quality when they do not have the same goals? In most organizations, one department does not even know what the other department's goals are! And they do not care. Why? Because they are not compensated to know, or evaluated to care. They are compensated and evaluated to care only about their own goals.

I once ran a division in a large company. The company was a so-called matrix organization, in that while each division was responsible for profit and loss, we all shared common manufacturing, markcting, and quality organizations. Manufacturing was supposed to support my division. But they were also supposed to support all the other divisions. And there was the inherent conflict: With limited resources, how could they choose which division to support?

And the other problem with manufacturing, just to use an example, it was not measured or compensated on divisional support. It was measured and compensated on its own goals such as lower cost, higher throughput, and lower inventory.

As a member of the so-called executive team in this company, I used to sit through marathon "beatings" (sorry, meant to say "meetings") where

	Organization Policies Aligned with Teams	Organization Policies Aligned against Teams
Hiring Policies	Team Interviews of candidates Psychological evaluation of candidates to determine team culture fit	Single Interviews, usually supervisor, not peers Candidates not screened for team fit
Compensation Policies	Pay for team results Incentive based upon achieving goal of budgeted company profit	Pay for individual results Incentive based upon achieving individual goals
Performance Evaluation Policies	Evaluation of team results Peer evaluation of performance	Evaluation of individual results Supervisor evaluation of performance
Goal Setting and Evaluation Policies	Goal #1 is achieving budgeted company profit	Goal #1 is individual or departmental goals
Communication Policies	Assumes everyone needs to know everything Monthly announcement of actual results to company profit goal	Assumes no one needs to know anything outside of their own function Does not communicate actual results except to a few top leaders

the president would demand better performance, and all his executives would throw blame at the other guys. All anyone wanted to do was get out of the room alive. Some team, huh?

This is very typical in organizations. They talk about teams, but they align all the organization policies against them.

WHAT DO TEAMS LOOK LIKE?

In order to create a team-oriented company, you have to have a clear model as a guide. Sometimes it is easier to describe something by first agreeing on what it is *not*. So let's begin by clearing up some misconceptions about teams.

Misconception #1: Teams Are Free of Conflict

Actually, it is quite the opposite. The best teams are not conflict-free. Without conflict, there can be no progress. Without conflict, teams can fall into "group-think," which blinds them to new, creative possibilities. Conflict is the tool great teams use to sharpen their perspectives, uncover flaws in their approaches, and create fresh, revolutionary thinking.

Every effective team has conflict. In a business world of limited resources and seemingly unlimited challenges, conflict is ever present. But most teams will pretend it does not exist, or just bury it from the boss's sight. They hope somehow it will just go away. People generally believe that conflict is not a good thing and that good teams do not have it, so they are afraid the boss will not be pleased if he or she found it.

I once led a team that pretended not to have conflict. In group meetings, everyone "made nice." They would not raise issues and they would pretend conflict did not exist. They would take potentially contentious issues "off-line," which meant the issues would not get dealt with at all.

Unresolved conflict never goes away on its own. Unresolved conflict festers and causes hard feelings among the team because they feel their opinions are not valued and their needs are not being met. So the idea is not to ignore conflict; the idea is to uncover it and teach teams how to manage it.

Knowing that conflict existed, but was not being addressed where it needed to be, which was at the senior leadership level, I would force it out. I would raise the contentious issues and would not let anybody out of the room until they were addressed. But more important, as the leader, I was letting them know that not only was conflict okay, but that I expected them to address it, not bury it.

Misconception #2: Teams Always Agree with Each Other

Actually, the worst thing you can have is team members always agreeing with each other. If your team members think you expect them to agree, you will be losing two of the most powerful attributes of a superstar team: originality and creative thought.

You want some of your team members to be "outliers," in that they bring offbeat thinking to the group. After all, some of the greatest advances (if not *all* the greatest advances) in the world resulted from outlier thinking. The key thing to remember is that when it is first introduced, an outlier is always a bad idea. Maybe it really *is* a bad idea, but you cannot know that until it is thoroughly examined.

When you reject an idea, the other thing to bear in mind is that rejection is only your opinion, not a fact. So you want your outliers to stick to their guns and be sure their ideas are thoroughly considered.

Be sure your teams know that not only is it okay not to agree, but that you expect disagreement. This is very important because if you do not tell them, most teams will not know it. They should strive for extraordinary results, not agreement for agreement's sake.

Misconception #3: Team Members Like Each Other

This is a good place to talk about how some of the other Values of Ingenuity™ are essential ingredients for great teams. Let's face fact, not everyone likes everyone else in this world. And the same is true in the workplace. If people happen to like each other on a team, so much the better. But that is not necessary. What is necessary is that they *respect* each other—the First Value of Ingenuity.

I have had many effective teams where the members did not like each other. But because they respected each other and were highly committed to the mission, they produced spectacular results. And I have been part of teams where I really disliked one of the other members, but respected their views and their ideas. In fact, some of the best ideas once came from a guy I did not like at all. And guess what? I do not think he liked me either, but he did respect me.

Always remember that *like* is not an essential ingredient in successful teams; *results* are.

Now let's examine the other side. What is a superstar team? There are many definitions of a team. Here is my own:

A team is a highly integrated, highly autonomous group of talented people highly committed to the team and each other in the pursuit of extraordinary results.

Sounds simple doesn't it? It is not. Let's look at each part of the definition.

"Highly integrated" means everyone on the team knows what everyone else is doing and is willing and anxious to help them. Unlike dysfunctional organizations where people work in a vacuum, not knowing or even caring what someone else is doing, in a high-performing company one hand always knows what the other is doing.

The success of one of my teams perfectly illustrates this concept. My team and I had just arrived in St. Louis for our industry's biggest trade show. We were excited to be there because we were ready to announce several new products that were sure to get the industry's attention. In fact, the future of our division rested on a successful launch at the show.

But when we got there, half of our products were stuck in transit and not likely to arrive in time. So what did I do? Actually, nothing. I didn't need to. The team huddled and doled out assignments to each other according to the talents and abilities of each member. One had the assignment of tracking down the products. Another had the assignment of getting duplicate products from the home office. Another had the assignment of re-configuring our trade show booth. And another was tasked with creating "virtual" representations that could be used if needed.

Now these guys were highly integrated. Highly autonomous. Highly committed. Now while this may be a simple example, it illustrates how this team nearly flawlessly executed on everything from product development to product delivery. Each one knew who would be best at a certain task, and then they executed against that.

At Miller Ingenuity, our factory teams see the orders every day. They make their own manufacturing plans based upon when the orders are due. They decide what orders have to be produced today, and if so, they produce and ship them. All without a boss telling them what to do. And if they learn a customer has an urgent need for a rush order, they move heaven and earth to make it happen. Highly autonomous. Highly committed.

Now that we have looked at what teams are, and what they are not, how do you go about creating a superstar team?

CREATING A TEAM ENVIRONMENT

A team-based framework does not just happen by itself. You need to take it in steps. Each step is as important as the others.

The first step toward creating a team environment is to understand that teams are not natural in organizations. They are *unnatural*. So if you want teamwork in your organization you have to create the framework for it. You cannot simply ask for it.

You would think that everyone would want to be part of a team. After all, many employees are deeply committed to their bowling teams. Don't all employees want to be part of a team? Well, actually no. Being part of a team is unnatural for employees, at least at the beginning. Most employees spend a lifetime in a work environment where they are individual contributors, not team players. You should not underestimate the ingrained cultural bias against teams.

Being part of a team, accountable to the team, and accountable for a result that is beyond an individual's control can be inherently uncomfortable. People ask themselves, "What happens if my teammate lets me down? What happens if the team can't reach its goal, but I can reach mine?"

Most employees naturally want to control their own destiny. To have to rely on someone else is not the way most of them have been trained and immersed over the course of their careers. And they are naturally skeptical about whether the whole team thing is a good idea.

Years ago, I developed a concept that I call "Team One" with all my executive teams. While the concept is quite simple, it is very difficult, if not impossible, for some people to accept. "Team One" is the senior leadership team. Its job is to run the overall company, not any specific function, even though each of them has a responsibility for certain functions. As an example, my sales vice president is expected to play on the senior leadership team. Yes, he runs the sales organization, but he plays on my team. I expect him to put the senior leadership team's needs ahead of the sales team's needs.

This is especially difficult for a sales guy to accept. By their very nature, sales people are lone wolves. So by the time a sales guy gets on the executive team, he has spent an entire career working on making the next deal. And when you ask him to forego that next deal for the good of the executive team, he just goes ballistic.

I once had a sales guy on my executive team who could not accept the idea when I first introduced it. Actually, he had a hard time even *understanding* the concept. He was bound by a career of devotion to short-term gains. To use a sports analogy, he was a professional golfer, not a member of a basketball team. I counseled him for months to get him to see the perspective and make the transition. He could not do it, so I asked him to leave. And you know what, he was happy to leave, because the whole team thing was totally against his nature. He was a good guy, but the team thing was not for him.

If you introduce teams in your organization, the concept will not work for many of your employees. You will have to help them understand, or, failing that, show them the door.

With the framework in place, you need the right people. Never just fill a vacant position with someone who is qualified on paper. Make sure that you hire only superstars who fit into the culture of your company and its teams. Hiring superstars is hard and it takes time. It also means hiring slow.

To make the best hiring choices I have always used peer interviewing, even in the factory. Why? To carefully build a team of superstars who want to work together. Excellence is contagious, and the senior leadership needs to make sure new candidates are a perfect fit with the culture, which makes blending into the team easier.

THE SIX PRINCIPLES YOU NEED TO CREATE SUPERSTAR TEAMS

Broadly speaking, all the policies and resources of the organization must support the team concept. If any of these are not in alignment, they will impede the development and maintaining of teams. They must all be synergistically in support of each other.

Make All Organization Goals Support the Key Metric, Which Is Profit

Perhaps the single most important thing you can do is get your goals aligned. Conflicting goals wreak havoc in organizations. They confuse the employees and create conflict. They destroy harmony and force people to compete against each other, rather than competing against the competition. They force people into a "me" and not "we" mindset.

The quality guys often have a goal of not letting anything out the back door, so they care only about meeting their goal of zero defects. The manufacturing guys want to shove everything out the back door no matter what the quality is, to meet their delivery goals. Sales guys want to meet their order goals without regard to the cost. Okay, maybe I am being a little facetious—but not much.

And I have seen so many companies where individual functions met their goals, yet they lost money! When Lehman Brothers went belly-up, many of the executives got big bonuses because they had made their individual goals, and yet the company went bankrupt. How insane is that?

Now I am not saying departments should not have their own goals. But they must be aligned with the only thing that matters at the end of the day: profit.

In every business I have run, all employees have had one major goal, and that was meeting the profit budget for the year. If we did not hit that number, nobody got kudos. And nobody got bonuses.

Align the Incentive Structure to Support Goal One

This is really very simple. If the company hits the budgeted profit number, everyone gets an incentive. If it doesn't, no one does, and I do not care how well you performed as a department. I like to say "no one gets the goodies if we don't hit the goal." Some people will not like this because that forces interdependence. But that is exactly what you want. You want people who will put the overall profit need above a departmental need.

It is a very powerful tool. Once a company I ran was in danger of not making the profit number. It was coming down to the last few weeks of the year. I was walking through the factory and one of the employees stopped me. He was very aware of "goal one" because we communicated how we were doing against budget every month, which is essential for this plan to work. He told me he knew it was going to be close and asked me if there was anything else he could do to hit the profit budget! Imagine that, a factory employee worried about the company making its profit budget. Now that is powerful!

Incorporate the Team into Your Hiring Practices

Once you have the team concept in place, the worst thing you can do is let anyone in the door that doesn't fit the profile of a good team player. You need to query candidates on their views toward teams. And do not simply ask them if they are a team player. What would you expect them to say?

Ask them related questions that might give you a clue. Here is a list I like to use:

- In places you have worked in the past, how was the workload decided?
- If there was an issue in your department, how did it get resolved?
- What was the best work environment in your career and why?
- What was the worst work environment in your career and why?
- When you think about the people you have worked with, were they generally helpful or not?
- What do you think is the best way to organize a department?
- In other places you worked, who had the best ideas?
- In other places you worked, how was conflict resolved?
- How would you describe your ideal workplace?

Listen very carefully to the answers. They will give you clues as to whether or not this person is a team player. Do not offer anything about your company first, lest you give them clues to the "right" answers.

The last essential is peer interviewing. Do not ever let anyone get on the team unless they pass muster with the teammates with whom they will work. They know best if the chemistry is right and whether or not the candidate would fit in.

Teach Team Conflict Resolution Techniques

As I said before, not only will effective teams have conflict, you *want* them to. But do not just throw them into the conflict pool and hope they can swim. Give them the tools they need. Here is a short list:

- Start by teaching them that conflict is not to be avoided. In fact, they should seek to uncover conflict and use it for the good of the team.
- Rule one in conflict resolution is respect for the other team members. Respect for them as people and respect for their ideas. No one gets to attack a member of the team.
- Train all members on how to facilitate discussions designed to bring out and deal with conflict. Teach them that conflict almost always has to be drawn out and will not appear magically. Some people have to be encouraged to make their opinions known, while others have to be toned down a bit because they want to dominate the discussion.
- Some conflict cannot be resolved by the team itself. Make sure they know and are comfortable with bringing a particularly sticky issue to a higher level in the organization.
- If as the leader you are not well versed in conflict resolution, get some expert help. A good industrial psychologist can help you with this.

Constantly Nurture and Protect the Team

Teams will not sustain themselves over time if they are not constantly nurtured and reinforced. There are several ways you can do this:

a) Celebrate the team's achievements at every chance you get. Do this publicly for all to see. I like to take out full-page ads in the local newspaper with pictures of the team and what it achieved. Everyone likes to see themselves in the paper and brag to their neighbors.

b) Reward the team at every chance you get. It does not have to be a lot of money (although it can be based upon the achievement). It can be something as simple as dinner out for the team and their spouses, or a pizza party thrown in their honor.

c) Celebrate the team's *failures* every chance you get. This may sound weird but it is an integral part of team nurturing. They need to know that failure is okay. The whole organization needs to know that failure is okay. Without failure there is no trying. Without trying there is no success. Let your teams fail without fear.

d) Do a team checkup from time to time. Individually, and as a group, ask them how they are doing. Ask them what is working well and what is not, and how you can help them make the team even better than it is.

e) Protect the team. To do this, sometimes you have to take a team member out. From time to time you will find that a team member is no longer suitable to be part of it. Often, the team themselves will tell you this. Do not let someone who has soured on the team idea infect the rest of the group. Ask them to leave the company. Once I had a consultant (whom I treated as a team member) try to throw my executive assistant under the bus by blaming her for not scheduling a meeting he missed. I do not know if she scheduled it or not, and I do not care. Because he blamed her, instead of supporting her I dismissed him. He was a valuable resource, but not as valuable as protecting my team.

Start by Building Your Own Team

As the leader, you have to build your own team before you can expect anyone else to do it. Too many leaders "expect from below what they are not willing to do above." Do not make the mistake of expecting team behavior from below when up high there is backstabbing left and right. Always remember that people in the organization are watching you all the time. They will take their cues from the top. So make sure the top gives the right cues.

Start by introducing the "Team One" concept to your senior leadership team. Do not underestimate the cultural impact this will have. It will likely be a huge shift in their mindset and require a retooling of how they have to be going forward. You will really need to sell the concept. You need to do this carefully and thoroughly.

Get some outside help to do a "Team One" check-up to see where the senior leaders stand on the concept and how receptive they are to it. This is not a one-hour exercise. Go off-site for a few days and really examine where you are and what the impact will be. This is very likely one of the most important things you will ever do. Do not make it a "check the box" exercise.

Any time I have done this I have engaged an industrial psychologist to facilitate and guide us through the process. Buckle up, because this process is probably going to involve a couple of really ugly days. But now is the time to understand and face the ugly truth. You do not want to walk away from that off-site without complete alignment.

Remember, if you do not get this right with the senior leaders, you have no chance in implementing it in the rest of the organization.

PROFILE: TOM SAWYER, WINONA STATE UNIVERSITY

At Winona State University in Winona, Minnesota, if you mention the name Tom Sawyer, folks will not think only of Mark Twain. They will think of their head football coach, a man who has positively impacted the lives of not only his student players but the wider community.

Sawyer has been the Winona State head coach since 1996 and is the winningest coach in Winona's football program history. He has guided the Warriors to 17 consecutive winning seasons, 5 NCAA Division II play-off appearances, and 3 Mineral Water Bowls, winning 2 of them. Among active NCAA Division II coaches, Sawyer is sixth in winning percentage and eighth in total victories.

The Winona State football program was not always that good. When Sawyer came on board in 1996, the playing field was called "the junkyard" and the team struggled to achieve winning seasons. But university president Dr. Darrell Krueger had assembled a Team One including himself, athletic director Larry Holstad, and coach Tom Sawyer. Together they spearheaded a successful effort to get the facilities upgraded. A multimillion-dollar facelift, which included a new artificial turf field and four-storey structure that serves as offices, suites, and game-day operations rooms, was built.

Sawyer also instills the value of giving back to the community and helping the less fortunate. His players continuously do community service work; even assisting in Nashville, Tennessee, with flood relief.

As Sawyer told me in an exclusive interview for the *American City Business Journals*, "WSU is committed to development of the stadium, facility and scholarships (which have expanded from seven to twenty-eight). I took your initiatives about toxic employees and changed some personnel. We also have the continued support of staff and administration plus the resources to hire the best."

"We focus more on execution and preparation than we do on the outcome. With approximately a hundred offensive plays per game, the players have repetitive decision-making over and over from a menu of options. Sometimes it fails, but it gives us the best chance to be successful. It's a percentage of success."

"From year to year, player turnover is just part of the game. We bring in around thirty-five new kids every year. For a full year we train them differently than the rest of the team; physically four days a week in the weight room, and two for the others. Mandatory study hours prepare them to become better student athletes."

I asked Sawyer about the concept of game momentum.

"Every unit that comes on the field has an opportunity for success or failure," he said. "If you go through the course of the game and you have a kick-off return, then the offense comes on the field and they do three positive things, but then they miss a field goal, then that missed field goal disrupts their momentum. We have to change or stalemate that momentum until another group comes on the field to continue or start new momentum. Once momentum is changed, the next group coming on wants to maintain it. That's where the mental training comes in."

How about analysis?

"We analyze every step they take in every play—every kid, every game, and every practice. If a player is supposed to step with his right foot then left foot, then go back and block back side, and instead he steps back before he goes forward, he's now two steps behind. The timing in that particular play is off. It's very important to fix every mistake, even if we win the game."

Since I am in the business of manufacturing, I asked him how CEOs can become more like coaches and less like managers.

"The biggest thing is the personal side of it," he said. "You have to know your people well, care deeply for them, and have a much higher expectation of them than they do. If I am the winningest coach in football, it's because I had one hundred and twelve guys doing it right most of the time."

PROFILE: PHIL COX, LEGACY FOOD STORAGE

Phil Cox is president and CEO of Legacy Food Storage, which prepares and markets food designed to be stored for up to 25 years without spoilage. Based in Salt Lake City, Utah, Legacy provides customers with convenient, pre-packaged, high-quality food to store for use during times of emergencies.

In an exclusive interview, Cox told me how he got involved in the business.

"My background is real estate and energy. As a family, we invested heavily in mixed-use, commercial, high-end and low-end residential real estate. We also owned Powder Mountain, a ski resort in northern Utah. When the market fell and hit bottom, real estate as a whole just disappeared. One morning a friend who had recently lost his job told me about e-commerce. The more he talked, the more interested I became, especially with my real estate background. I have a pretty good idea of the cost of building out a retail center. When I learned the cost of building an e-commerce platform, I recognized it's substantially less expensive."

"Fascinated by it, I suggested we get into e-commerce together, believing it might be much easier—and much more profitable—than launching a brick-and-mortar business. We launched our first Legacy site in January 2011 and went from roughly $18,000 in revenue to more than $300,000 by March. I thought we'd hit the jackpot. Then reality kicked in. As an e-commerce reseller, we shot past our primary supplier's ability to keep up with demand. Because of this, I had to learn how to produce my own goods."

"Typically, my business style is a partnership with successful people. I find really talented people who are the best at what they do. Personally, I am not a bright enough individual to do everything by myself. I'm sure there are many who can, but I am not one of them."

"I help people become better off and treat them well in the process. I believe that what prevents people from being successful are their own restrictions on their abilities. I help others accomplish their goals, which in turn helps me accomplish my goals. I'm a capitalist. I believe everybody wants to make money."

But this does not mean that short-term cash considerations dictate how Cox runs the business.

"I actually fired the person initially making revenue for my company because he was toxic to the business for long-term success," he told me. "We replaced him with the best, thus making us even more money. The idea is to not allow fear to run your business. We've had to make hard decisions that might look stupid, but are necessary, and the best option in the long term. We always move upward."

I asked him about his business model.

"One thing I'd like to clarify," said Cox. "People think we're in food storage. We're not, at least not exclusively. We are in e-commerce. We'll be going into nutritional products, camping food and textiles, expecting to double and triple revenue every few years like we are doing now. We're in the business of making money."

Assembling the best possible team of smart people, being innovative, and keeping your goals focused on the long term are important keys to success.

SEVEN

The Fourth Value of Ingenuity—Community

Community is a value that contributes not only to the strength and performance of a company, but benefits the outside world as well. It is one of the rare values that cuts both ways, both inside and outside the company. And each way that it cuts reinforces the other. That is why community is such a powerful value.

The human need for a sense of community is well documented. Since the dawn of time, people, neighborhoods, nations, and whole societies have turned to communities as a primary vehicle for fulfilling the basic human needs of belonging, integration, and fulfillment of needs and shared emotional connections. There can be no doubt that communities have a great impact on society. This impact can be both positive and negative.

What about community in the workplace? What does it mean, and what does it look like?

Here is an academic definition of workplace community, quoted by Neal Chalofsky in the *Organizational Development Journal*: "A great workplace is one in which you trust the people you work for, have pride in what you do, and enjoy the people you are working with. The elements of a great workplace culture are . . . credibility, respect, fairness, pride and camaraderie."

Here is another one by Rob Goffee and Gareth Jones in "Creating the Best Workplace on Earth" in the *Harvard Business Review*:

Create an authentic environment before managers can be effective leaders through their prescribed steps:

Let people be themselves.
Unleash the flow of information.
Magnify people's strengths.
Stand for more than shareholder value.
Show how the daily work makes sense.
Have rules people can believe in.

Here is one more definition, from Ian Gee and Matthew Hanwell in *The Workplace Community: A Guide to Releasing Human Potential and Engaging Employees*:

> By workplace communities, we do not mean people sitting around in a circle fighting over who is going to get the talking stick next! We mean, a structured and planned way by which people have the opportunity to contribute outside of the traditional hierarchy and silos of organization. Engaging with each other in very different ways, and in doing so creating extraordinary results. We believe workplace communities, if implemented with diligence and care, can unleash latent talent, capability, and capacity in the organization and have a positive impact on business results.

In the context of The 7 Values of Ingenuity™, the word *community* has a dual meaning.

It means both the *internal* company community and the *external* local community.

The internal company community and the external local community are inextricably linked, or at least they should be. Linking the two dramatically increases the effectiveness of the company.

However you define *company community*, the definition, in the real business world, is much less important than establishing a working corporate culture that synergizes with the other values in place and, most important, *contributes to the profitability of the company*.

THE POSITIVE CORPORATE COMMUNITY

Academics can debate and refine their definitions of what corporate community is, and what it is not. In the corporate world, you and I have to *bring it to life*—we do not have time to perfect definitions.

While researchers can attempt to define what a community is, they fall short in prescribing how one might purposefully *create* a community. The fact is that communities often form quite by accident. While an accidental community might very well serve the needs of its members, it does not necessarily serve the needs of society at large. In fact, often they do not. While some communities have no significant impact on the world around them (*ambivalent* communities), others have great impact. In fact, many communities actually adversely impact the world around them as *negative* communities. These communities negatively impact others because they are concerned only with the needs of their members. And their members, on the whole, are not concerned with the needs of those outside the community.

On the other hand, a *positive* corporate community benefits both the company and the larger outside world.

There is a strong business case for building and maintaining a positive corporate community as one of your core values. I have witnessed the power of positive corporate communities first hand, by creating them in every company I have ever managed. I have also seen the debilitating impact that toxic corporate communities can have on the health of the company. These observations have not come from studying others, or from academic research. They have come from living through them and observing the impact they have on profit, or on loss, as the case may be. They came from trial and error, until I discovered what worked in creating effective corporate communities and what did not.

Why is a positive community important? At the most fundamental level, employees want to get satisfaction from their work and their roles in the outside community. If employees feel the company is supporting the external communities where they live and that they care about, internal satisfaction goes up. An employee who is satisfied with the company community is more likely to be satisfied with the external community.

An added benefit is the external community is enriched by the company's and its employees' efforts not only in money but also in volunteerism. What could be better than higher profits and better communities because of those higher profits? Sound like an unattainable nirvana? Hardly; I have witnessed it over and over.

A POSITIVE COMMUNITY STRENGTHENS A COMPANY'S PERFORMANCE

Let's start with how the value of community strengthens the performance of the company. Just as in the external communities, people inside a company want to feel like they *belong* there. But in some organization cultures, belonging to the community is an elusive and sometimes unattainable goal.

The negative community is closed-minded to new arrivals. The rituals, beliefs, and habits of the negative community are not intended to be knowable to an outsider or a new recruit. Obstacles are placed in the way of someone attempting to be accepted and a part of the community. The community asserts the new recruit has to earn their way in. And once earned, the community wants the new recruit to feel like it was the attainment of a monumental achievement, reserved for a few special people. In some organization communities, this is all part of the mystique, and these communities feel it is important to maintain this mystique.

Think back to any time you began with a company as a new employee. How did you feel? Anxious, uncertain, overwhelmed? Probably all of those things, but on a basic level your primary concern was: "Will I fit in here?" So what did you do? You took your cues from the community of other employees and learned what it takes to fit in.

When an employee joins a company, he or she can feel a lot like a new recruit into a closed society like Scientology or a college fraternity. The standards of behavior, rituals, rules, and customs (all of which form a community) can be secretive and difficult to get accustomed to.

As a company leader, that is exactly what you *don't* want.

What you want is an open-minded, open-ended community that is welcoming and inclusive. Not only does that enable better performance over the long run, but eliminates all the wasted time and anxiety (read: poor performance) that new recruits might otherwise be exposed to. You want new hires to be able to hit the ground running on day one. You do not want them to take weeks or months to get acclimated.

Once they have felt their way around, which can take months or even years, the new recruit may discover it is not the kind of community they wanted to join at all. And what happens then? One of two things: They either leave the company, in which case you are burdened with the lost productivity and costs of replacing them; or what is worse, they stay and are perpetually dissatisfied with the community.

Their dissatisfaction drives everything from poor productivity to higher costs. But the most detrimental result is that the dissatisfied recruit begins to *infect the rest of the community*. A form of cognitive dissonance comes into play, and the new recruit feels compelled to defend his or her negative view of the community and convince others that their positive view of the company community is wrong.

If you are a new recruit in a positive community, there is no doubt, from day one, what the community is like. Your community should be an open book. Everyone should know what it *feels* like to be part of it. Any one of your employees should be able to explain to a new recruit what it *means* to be part of the community. What it *feels like* and *what it means* are the cornerstones of a strong value of community inside a company.

As a leader, you have to take an active role in defining your community. Assuming you have a community by design, not default, whatever your internal community is, whatever attributes it has, you only want to invite people into it who believe in what the community believes in. You only want to invite people into it who want to belong to your kind of community. You only want to invite people who will contribute to the community, and be satisfied that their needs are met by it. Otherwise cognitive dissonance infection will jeopardize it.

WHAT COMMUNITY FEELS LIKE TO THE NEW RECRUIT

Imagine you are that new recruit again. You have just finished your first day at your new job and you just got home. Chances are, your spouse will ask you, "How was your first day?"

Your answer might be "good," "bad," "okay," or possibly "confusing." All of these answers are subjective answers based upon how you felt that first day. It would be too early to make an objective judgment based upon quantifiable data, such as the number of widgets you produced that day. That may come later, but your initial assessment of a company will be a subjective judgment of how you felt about its community.

Were your coworkers generally helpful and interested in on-boarding you? Or did they shut you out and leave you on your own? Or perhaps they were somewhere in the middle, giving you what they were told to, but not much more. Did you feel uneasy, or were you comfortable being there?

In 1970, I was a United States Navy recruit fresh out of boot camp. I had traveled halfway around the world to join my first ship. To say that I felt anxious and uncertain would be an understatement. I was excited and terrified at the same time. I could not wait to find out how, or even if, I would fit in.

Shortly after I boarded the ship I was shepherded upstairs to meet the boss—in my case, he was the chief petty officer in charge of the engine room, where I was assigned to work. When I was introduced to him he said, "Hoss, what took you so long to get here?"

I never did get the feeling that he welcomed my presence on the ship. And I did not make up the "hoss" reference. Forty-six years later, I still remember exactly what he said! That should give you some idea as to the power of a fresh recruit's first introduction to the community. Right then and there I would have quit that community if I could have. So what did I do instead? I was perpetually dissatisfied and I spent the next several years trying to change the community to fit my vision of the world.

As I said earlier, it is a win-win if you can create an internal community that strengthens both the company and the external community. And done right, the effort in strengthening the external community reinforces the company community. In fact, I would argue you should not engage in any community building efforts unless they do both. One way to do this is by engaging your employees in community service work that requires them to work in teams, which is another one of your core 7 Values of Ingenuity™.

At Miller Ingenuity, we provide plenty of opportunities for this, but one of my favorites is the Adopt-a-Highway program. Miller has adopted a one-mile section of one of the highways in town, and we are responsible for keeping it clean and clutter free. Our employees decide when it is time to go and clean it. They decide which day and time they will go and arrange their production work schedule to accommodate it. When they get to the highway they work in self-directed teams to get the job done, just like they do at work. They do this without missing a beat in meeting the needs of our customers.

When they are done they feel pride in ownership of their section of the highway, just like they feel pride in ownership of their work at Miller. Their external community work for Adopt-a-Highway reinforces the internal community by reinforcing the team value.

The bond between them, as teammates and internal community members, strengthens every time they clean their portion of the highway. This is especially useful if the highway team members are *not* in a team together in the company.

Whenever they have done their stint on the highway, I take out a half-page four-color ad in the local paper featuring a picture of them and their section of the highway. They tell their neighbors and friends that that particular stretch of highway is their responsibility, and tell them how they just beautified it.

This simple example illustrates perfectly how the internal and external communities support each other.

Let's assume for a moment that you do not buy the argument that external community efforts build strong and vibrant internal communities. You may ask whether corporations should put effort or dollars into the external community at all.

On this, there are two schools of thought.

One is that corporations should be concerned with the production of only profit and the health of the enterprise. Proponents of this school say that funneling profit dollars to the external community for any purpose is not related to the production of profit and should be avoided. They would argue that philanthropy and external community building is the legitimate role of government, not business. And besides, they argue, the shareholders of the company, not the managers, should decide if that is how they wish to employ the profit that has been returned to them in the form of dividends.

This argument misses several critical points.

1. Shareholders are often widely dispersed geographically and may not have a sense of what is needed by the communities within which the company operates.
2. Shareholders often do not have an appreciation for the value that strong external communities bring to the enterprise. If they do not value it, they are unlikely to use dividend dollars to support it.
3. Shareholders are often constrained in providing community service by virtue of not living in the communities in which their company operates.

A bond between the workplace and external communities satisfies both arguments. The company gets as much back from contributing to the community as it gives. The dollars a company provides to the external community, *if employed properly*, actually produce profit. But the dollars have to be employed in a synergistic way that strengthens the internal operations of the company. To simply give money to the community may feel good, and may actually do good, but misses the purpose of a rational enterprise—to either produce profit or provide effective services to its members.

Another critical point this argument misses is that government alone is not able to provide for the total needs of a community. And let's face it, the company will pay for this one way or the other, either in philanthropy or income tax dollars. Philanthropy dollars are not only much more efficient, but can be employed more quickly and effectively when the need arises.

THE RUSHFORD FLOOD AND THE COMPANY GOLF OUTING

Here is a case in point. The town of Rushford lies just outside of Winona, where Miller Ingenuity's corporate headquarters is located. In 2007, Rushford suffered a devastating flash flood that wiped out half the town. Many people lost their homes and businesses. The town's fresh water supply was destroyed. Electricity was out for weeks. It was a disaster.

The government had a legitimate role in crisis recovery. It set about rescuing people who were stranded in their homes, it tended to the sick and injured, and it eventually restored fresh water and electricity.

But the government could not quickly target food and water to the affected residents. The government had its rules, regulations, and bureaucracy to satisfy, and that took time.

Miller Ingenuity made an immediate decision, and within a day we had deployed cash, supplies, and people to the aid of the residents of Rushford. The Miller Ingenuity volunteers were members of our internal community who were not only willing but eager to help the external community. Our employees did everything from packing boxes with food to delivering medical supplies.

There is no doubt that this effort diluted the production of Miller's profit during the days and weeks we were involved in the Rushford relief effort. And one might argue that since most of our employees were not from that community, we should not have been involved at all.

But several of our employees were Rushford residents. One of them, Jesse Smith, lost everything. He and his family lost their house and all their possessions. Jesse was a young guy, with a young wife and very young children. They did not have much in the bank. And while insurance may have replaced the house, it was unlikely Jesse could have afforded any more coverage than would have satisfied the holder of the mortgage. For Jesse and his family, this was a life-changing event. He had no idea where to turn for financial aid. But his Miller Ingenuity community did.

Several weeks after the flood, I was walking through the factory and a group of employees approached me. They said they had been thinking about how they could help Jesse. They had already given what money they could afford, but they felt more needed to be done. And they had an idea.

Now just imagine that—a group of employees who are thinking about how to help one of their own. Let's just take a quick sidebar time-out. If you have an internal community that is self-aware (aware that one of their own is in need) and concerned about its members, do you think that contributes to the strengthening of the enterprise? And if people in your internal community are concerned about one another *personally*, do you think they might be concerned about each other *professionally*?

Absolutely.

The employees' idea was to cancel the annual company golf outing and give the money it would have cost to Jesse and his family. To put it in context, every employee looks forward to this outing. They get the day off with pay (whether they come to the outing or not), golf, beer, prizes and awards, and a steak dinner, all on the company. Now, I have seen some snake-pit factories whose employees would not give that up to save their mothers! But our employees said they would not feel right about having a golf party while a member of their community was suffering.

Let's take another sidebar time-out. What do your employees talk about when they are at work? Oh, I suppose maybe a little politics, current events around town, and perhaps what is going on in their personal lives. But in negative internal communities, they tend to talk about how they dislike each other. Or how one group is not pulling their weight, or how horrible the boss is. Negative communities focus on the negative aspects of their corporate and community life. In contrast, positive internal communities focus on the well-being of the community. That is exactly what this group of employees was doing the day they approached me.

So we canceled the golf outing and provided to Jesse the amount it would have cost the company. It was not that much money to the company—only about $8,000. But it was a godsend to Jesse and his family. And as a matter of fact, I considered providing Jesse with the money and having the golf outing too. But that would have diluted the power of the sacrifice his community made for him. And therefore, it would have diluted the power of the community. So I didn't.

We asked Jesse and his wife to come to the company so we could give them something. They had an idea we might be giving them money, but they had no idea the whole idea was generated by his coworkers. I gathered all the employees together for the event. Then I told the story of how Jesse's coworkers wanted to help him and hatched this "kill the golf outing" idea. When I presented Jesse's wife with the check, she wept.

I could have just mailed a check. I could have just given the check to Jesse without all the pomp and circumstance. But then I would have missed a golden opportunity to massively reinforce the community. As a leader, you should never miss an opportunity to reinforce the spirit of your community.

The moment was an emotional one. And the emotion of that moment reinforced the Miller Ingenuity community in a way no amount of money or speeches could. It reinforced our community in a way no slogan or banner on the wall ever could. Strong emotions make for strong communities, and strong emotional moments generate strong stories. Our employees still tell that story with pride. I still tell that story with pride.

You might think this was an isolated event, and not necessarily part of the Miller Ingenuity community DNA. You'd be wrong. Several years later another employee lost everything in a fire. What do you think our employees did? You guessed it, the same thing they did after the Rushford floods. They canceled the golf outing and came to the aid of a community member in need.

THE IMPORTANCE OF COMMUNITY

I know that now and in the future, the quality of my workforce is totally dependent on a strong community. (If you will recall from Chapter 1, one of the five key conditions for manufacturing to flourish is a source of high-quality labor.) The future of a workforce, and therefore future of any company, depends on operating in communities with quality education, healthcare, and what I call a "strong social infrastructure." By that I mean a community with a low crime rate, a rich ethnic and cultural diversity, and a high work ethic.

These community attributes do not happen naturally, and often governments are constrained in their efforts to bring about and sustain these qualities. That is why private enterprise should play a role.

Here are some key ideas on how you can create an effective workplace community of your own.

Create Community with a Clearly Defined Mission and Purpose

What's the primary purpose of your bowling team? It's pretty simple: To win games.

What are the secondary purposes of your bowling team? Also simple: To have fun, enjoy the camaraderie, and perhaps raise some money for charity.

A company's community should be purposeful, and the purpose needs to relate to the goals of the enterprise. The primary aim of an internal community must be to enable the enterprise to produce profit. An internal community should be *effective*—it should behave in such a way as to minimize what I call "community distractions."

Community distractions are activities that take away from the primary purpose of the community. These distractions include:

- When the members are confused as to the mission and reason for the existence of the community. This can happen when the leaders send out mixed, confusing, or even worse, no signals as to the purpose of the community. It is critical that the leaders constantly reinforce the mission and purpose of the community. Otherwise employees spend too much time thinking about and discussing how they fit in with each other.
- When community members engage in activity that does not support the mission, purpose, and goals of the organization. The biggest danger here is that employees might *join or form another community* that is not aligned with the organization's mission. A labor union is a perfect example of this.
- When the community morphs into a quasi-social organization. Company bowling leagues are a good example of how this can occur. I am not against bowling leagues, but I have seen companies that have leagues for every kind of activity you can think of. Their goal is to engage all employees in the social-league activities in hopes that will bond them together to make them more productive. It won't; it will just make them more social away from the workplace.

As a leader, you have to limit the number and nature of community distractions. You have to strike a balance between zero social activities and so many activities that the mission of the community becomes blurred. I once worked for a company that had leagues for bowling, tennis, golf, swimming, softball, baseball, running—the list went on. Not only did this create community distractions, it created employee dissatisfaction. People were dissatisfied that the leagues were not run right, or they did not offer enough, or the company did not pay enough of the cost. You get the picture. Do not make the mistake of believing multiple leagues can be surrogates for effective workplace communities. Leagues can cost money and create dissatisfaction.

Establish Leaders Who Are Community Enabled

This is an important part of the process. If you do not get this down right, nothing else you do will matter. And the best part of establishing community-enabled leaders is they will also be terrific leaders in general.

Everyone knows "command and control" died in the 1970s, but not every leader got the word. You need leaders who reject command and control. That is clear. But you also need leaders who are comfortable in relinquishing *almost all control* to the community.

COMMUNICATE WITH EMPLOYEES

You cannot just pop-up a banner on the wall and create some clever slogans around the word *community*. Leaders need to clearly articulate to employees what it means, and why it is important to them. As in every occasion of employee communication, I advocate telling the truth. Do not try to mask the real purpose of building a community.

You should use relentlessly simple communication in all matters, but especially in this one. Be relentless. Do not just talk about it once. Talk about it constantly, relentlessly. And keep it very simple.

As your community matures, the members of the community will suggest and initiate social activities, which is a sign the community is maturing. As an example, at Miller Ingenuity, recently our community decided to organize a monthly potluck lunch in the cafeteria. This is a perfect community activity because it facilitates communication, camaraderie, and teamwork.

PROFILES: CLICK RAIN AND THE HAL LEONARD GROUP

There is perhaps no better example of the value of community than Click Rain. In a nutshell, Click Rain helps companies find the right mix of online tools and strategies to make an impact on the web. Sounds pretty mundane, doesn't it?

Hardly. Since CEO Paul Ten Haken launched his online marketing company in 2008, company revenues have skyrocketed by over 1,300 percent. For three consecutive years, *Inc. 5000* named Click Rain as one of America's fastest-growing private companies. Notice the company was started in the middle of the great recession of 2008!

I interviewed Paul as part of my "League of Extraordinary CEOs" series in the *American City Business Journals*. Paul told me as part of that interview that a big competitive advantage is the culture he developed at Click Rain. He told me that he has invested more of his time and money into the culture than anything else.

"Annually," he told me, "we invest a lot of money in our people. For instance, we give our employees an extra week of paid time off every year if they use it for an international service trip. This year, I had nine employees go overseas for mission or service work, and we paid half of the cost. We've removed two of the huge barriers that people often have to do that sort of thing: time and money."

So Click Rain supports the worldwide community with its time, its money, and its people. Just imagine if every company gave time off and paid half the cost for nine people to do mission or service work. Imagine how much better of a world this would be!

But we are all in the business to make profit, and the link between Click Rain's community-minded culture and the bottom line is clear. You don't get on the *Inc.5000* list if it is not.

"By making that investment in the employees," said Paul, "Our clients and prospective employees notice. Our employees come back more energized and refreshed than from any conference I could send them to, and they're also more appreciative of our investment."

Keith Mardak is chairman and CEO of the world's largest music publishing company, Hal Leonard Group. When I interviewed Keith as part of the League series, I could not help but be impressed not only with his company but his civic and community mindedness.

The success of the company is astounding, especially considering how the music publishing industry has changed in a digital world. But even more astounding is how Keith pays it forward by giving back to the community.

He is a big supporter of the Boys and Girls Clubs of greater Milwaukee, having served 43,000 children in one year alone. And he does this personally. Corporately, Hal Leonard sponsors the Milwaukee Symphony Pop Series, the Hal Leonard Young Musicians Program, and a number of other programs aimed at enriching the lives of the community.

I asked him why philanthropy was important to him. He said, "I feel it's only right to share what you have with those who are less fortunate."

A positive company community can both impact your bottom line and make a difference to your customers and neighbors.

EIGHT

The Fifth Value of Ingenuity—Commitment

A commitment is a binding pledge that obligates you to carry out a course of action or reach a goal. Making a commitment to what you do—whether in your personal life or your professional life—is a fundamental principle of success.

Commitments are serious, affecting your thoughts, actions, and communication. Adverse to a half-hearted attempt, a commitment means that you try as hard as you can, you do not look back, and you resolve to find solutions to problems. Quitting is never an option.

It takes commitment, from the top down, for a company to be truly ingenious. It takes making brave decisions and, what's more, sticking with them, even if things get worse before they get better. Change is never easy, but if organizations are made aware of the benefits of change, they can more easily commit to those changes and do a better job of implementing them.

Your stakeholders—employees, vendors, stockholders, lenders—look for commitment at every level of your company, and especially in the corner office. What are the characteristics of your personal commitment to your company? There are many; here are three.

1. Motivation. The leader who is committed does not need motivation to perform their job. Have you ever heard a leader say, "I'd enjoy doing this job even if no one paid me?" That is commitment. It is why people say that when you love what you do, it is not like work. Unmotivated people are content to collect a paycheck instead of taking personal responsibility for their piece of the work. To achieve your future goals, it is extremely important to motivate yourself; or find work someplace else.

2. Leadership. A truly committed business leader is able to display strong leadership even during hard times. When there is a tough situation, there are entrepreneurs who are too happy to blame others—the meddling government, China, the lousy local schools, high taxes, whatever. When plans are not going as expected, genuine leaders accept it, step up and assume responsibility. As the person who bears ultimate responsibility, you have to shift the business back on track.

3. Ambition. Committed leaders project confidence and ambition, not introversion. They push themselves and their employees toward a goal, and if it looks like they are not going to reach it, they push a little harder. A leader who is not ambitious has no desire to work hard toward the company's success. An ambitious leader understands that failure is part of a learning curve and carries on to reach the goal.

A leader displays his or her commitment in many ways. They include:

- Always pursuing the goal, even when stressed.
- Investing time, money, and energy to reach the preferred outcome.
- Remaining focused and determined, even in adversity, to reach the main objective.
- Rejecting short-term plans for long-term strategies that will fulfill the ultimate goal.
- Applying resourcefulness, creativity, and ingenuity to solve any issues that would stymie achieving the goal.

MISTAKES TO AVOID

Commitment is especially important during times of major change, such as acquiring another company. One of the biggest and most tragic mistakes CEOs and boards make is over-committing by absorbing big companies that they ultimately cannot digest. We all know about the massive premiums paid in the high-tech and social media sectors.

For example, consider Amazon.com. The company that is becoming a global colossus posted its very first profits in the fourth quarter of 2014. Remember, Amazon had been founded 20 years earlier—and had operated for *20 years* without showing a profit! Amazon's business model is defined by "spend money to make money," except what operating profits they do post are pretty skimpy, and big losses of hundreds of millions of dollars have been commonplace.

Amazon has expanded by making dozens of acquisitions—some of them very big. In 2009, Amazon paid $850 million for shoe retailer Zappos. In 2014, Amazon bought the video game platform Twitch for a billion dollars, while simultaneously expanding its same-day delivery service across the United States and launching a phone that consumers did not want.

Operating at negative margins cannot last forever and present a major obstacle to prospective competitors. Many believe that Amazon is planning price hikes in anticipation of its competitors going under. The question is, how much longer can Amazon afford to spend, acquire, and expand before shareholders—the people who back the company with their own money—decide that Amazon looks more like a pumpkin than a royal carriage?

It is what I call "swelling" a company—not growing it.

Be careful not to over commit. Being very selective to the opportunities that present themselves on a regular basis is extremely important. Your time and attention is limited, so only commit to the most viable choices.

We must also recognize that commitments often have limitations—and you have to be tough and realistic when considering changing your commitment. If something is not working that you committed to, you could just make excuses rather than admit defeat. Don't. Accept that a change needs to be made in spite of your best efforts.

Commitments must be reviewed as your business grows and your personal life and priorities change. It is natural that loyalties may shift and resources could vary, so it is important to revise commitments that are no longer feasible.

Commitments often require resources—time, money, manpower. Be absolutely honest with yourself when making a commitment that you actually have the required time and resources to fulfill the promise. It is possible you may have to give up something else in exchange.

KNOW YOUR ADVERSARY: "MADE IN CHINA 2025"

Every manufacturer in the United States needs to remember that long-term commitment to your goals is an important key to success. Why? Because our biggest adversaries are committed to sustained, long-term growth. They are taking the long view, and so must you.

In America, we are making great strides in advanced manufacturing, which is resulting in lower costs and higher productivity. We are turning the tide, but China is not sitting idly by as we get further into Manufacturing 2.0. Nearly 80 percent of China's economy is tied to manufacturing; so to maintain its competitive position, China is striving to make manufacturing productivity improvements.

China is making a renewed commitment to manufacturing. Are we?

In May 2015, China unveiled its "Made in China 2025" campaign, a 10-year national plan to bolster China's competitiveness in the manufacturing sector through automation and overall improvement in technology. The plan was approved by China's Central Cabinet, headed by Premier Li Keqiang.

"Made in China 2025" was formulated as China faced higher international competition, declining manufacturing demand and lower financial gains.

According to a report by China Daily Information Co. (CDIC), China's 2025 plan focuses on "improving manufacturing innovation, integrating technology and industry, strengthening the industrial base, fostering Chinese brands, enforcing green manufacturing, and promoting breakthroughs in ten key sectors."

Commenting on the plan, Miao Wei, minister of industry and information technology (MITT) said, "By 2025, China will basically realize industrialization nearly equal to the manufacturing abilities of Germany and Japan at their early stages of industrialization."

The United States is not specifically mentioned—but you know the top dog is always the top target.

Following the 10-year plan are an additional 2 plans, which intend to make China a prominent manufacturing force by 2049; the People's Republic of China's 100th anniversary.

Their main objectives are innovation in manufacturing improvement; incorporating industry and information technology; reinforcing the industrial base; promoting China's own brands; green manufacturing enforcing; manufacturing restructure advancement; supporting service-oriented manufacturing plus manufacturing-related service industries; manufacturing internationalizing, and promoting breakthroughs in 10 key industrial sectors.

These are the key industrial sectors targeted for breakthroughs according to China's 2025 plan:

1. New information technology
2. Numerical control tools and robotics
3. Aerospace equipment

4. Ocean engineering equipment and high-tech ships

5. Railway equipment

6. Energy saving and new energy vehicles

7. Power equipment

8. New materials

9. Biological medicine and medical devices

10. Agricultural machinery

Here at Miller Ingenuity, we take particular note of item number five on China's hit list: railway equipment.

To which we say, "Bring it on!"

China will initiate a barrage of new rules to intensify established improvements to move their plan forward.

"There are many criteria to judge whether a country is a manufacturing power or not, including industrial scale, optimized industrial structure, sound quality and efficiency and sustainable development; but the key lies in innovation," said Li Beiguang, deputy head of MIIT planning division.

Innovation—does the word sound familiar?

Chinese manufacturing accounts for about 20 percent of the world's total, and in the United States we tend to see it as monolithic and formidable. But according to Li Beiguang, Chinese manufacturing is "far from strong."

According to the CDIC, "The 2025 plan will span the whole manufacturing industry, applying advanced ideas not only from Germany and Japan, but also from the United States and Britain, among others, said officials."

Will those "advanced ideas" actually be "advanced stolen ideas?" No company in America can afford to think otherwise. Has your company invested in cyber security? No? Nowadays, not having sufficient cyber security is like leaving your front door unlocked when you go out at night. Would you leave your front door unlocked so that a thief could walk in and steal your stuff? Of course not. Likewise, you need to secure your digital data and keep it safe from theft or sabotage. The Chinese will try to get the information they want in any way possible—so do not make it easy for them.

As a small or mid-sized manufacturer, you may not be able to influence government policy. But you can—and must—understand the value of commitment to long-term success. Why? Because you can bet your competitors—the ones that are across the ocean as well as across the street—are taking it very seriously.

WALMART'S COMMITMENT TO U.S. MANUFACTURING

Americans have a love-hate relationship with Walmart, the nation's biggest private employer and purveyor of just about every type of retail merchandise imaginable. A typical Walmart store stocks 120,000 items, and in the popular imagination, most of these items come straight off the freighters from China.

It is not quite that simple, but you cannot deny that the American consumer's relentless demand for more and more consumer goods at lower and lower prices has impacted U.S. manufacturing.

Walmart has become sensitive to both the reality and the perception of the corrosive effects of continued offshoring of manufacturing. Since the Great Recession, the retail giant has made a new commitment to U.S. manufacturing.

During the 2014 U.S. Manufacturing Summit, Walmart said, "It can create more American jobs by supporting more American manufacturing. Jump-starting the manufacturing industry and rebuilding the middle class requires a national effort by companies, industry leaders, lawmakers, and others. By making production more affordable and feasible in the United States, Walmart can bring our customers more U.S.-made products, and manufacturers can create more jobs in America."

According to Walmart, and perhaps contrary to popular belief, data from Walmart suppliers indicates that about two-thirds of what customers spend at Walmart are on made-in-America products. Walmart believes more can be done.

"By investing in products that support American jobs," says Walmart, "we are able to bring new products to our shelves that our customers want—and new jobs to our communities. Increasing domestic manufacturing will help create additional jobs in the U.S., and that's good for American businesses. The time is right to bring manufacturing back to the United States. Overseas labor costs are rising while energy costs in the U.S. are low. It just makes sense to build things closer to the point of consumption. America is where the innovation is happening."

There is that word again—*innovation*!

"We have over 1,300 product categories and we're evaluating every one of them," says Walmart. "We have five hundred active initiatives on certain products in categories including light bulbs, tires, bicycles, home textiles, toys, pets, cookware, and many more."

"Some categories and certain products are more ready to be re-shored. They share similar characteristics including accessible raw materials, highly automated production, and high transportation costs, and are impacted by seasons or trends. ... Our modeling suggests the U.S. can offer very competitive manufacturing options, especially given many rising cost variables overseas."

Walmart spokeswoman Kayla Whaling told Kim Souza of *The City Wire*, "We continue to see the fruits of this initiative come through." As examples of Walmart suppliers that are expanding U.S. manufacturing, *The City Wire* reported that True Science Holdings, makers of pet care products, is introducing a new pet treats line under Betsy Farms, VetIQ, and Delightibles brands that will create 200 new jobs.

"Working with True Science, Walmart is able to bring customers quality pet products while also helping create American jobs," said Michelle Gloeckler, senior vice president of U.S. Manufacturing at Walmart. "An increase in U.S.-made products for our customers helps manufacturers create more jobs here in America."

Since 1949, NUK USA, the maker of baby pacifiers, has assembled its products in the United States. With a commitment from Walmart, they will expand their U.S. facility by moving a portion of their manufacturing in Europe to Wisconsin, giving customers the opportunity of choosing pacifiers that are "Made in the U.S.A."

Andover Healthcare, founded in 1976 in Salisbury, Massachusetts, will expand business to Portsmouth, New Hampshire. There they will manufacture cohesive bandages for Walmart, in their new 52,000 square foot facility.

KENT INTERNATIONAL

While I am on the subject of Walmart, the story of Kent International shows how commitment makes a difference to long-term success.

Arnold Kamler, chairman and CEO of Kent International, Inc., a high-volume, mass-market bike supplier to Walmart, Toys R Us, Target, and other retailers, is a third-generation bicycle guy whose grandfather Avram had emigrated from Poland a century earlier and set up a small shop on New York City's Lower East Side.

Avram Kamler started small, repairing bikes in his little shop. His son Phillip grew the business and moved it to New Jersey; this was at a time when the United States had hundreds of competing bicycle producers. In 1958, he changed the company name to Kent International.

Avram's grandson Arnold Kamler inherited a big challenge. When he joined the business in 1972, there were eight American bicycle manufacturers and about forty bicycle importers. Eventually, the eight American companies that were manufacturing had abandoned the field, and of the forty importers, only Kent and Raleigh still remain today.

By 1979, the bicycles that were coming from Taiwan were becoming more expensive, and China was not yet ready to compete. So Kent began to assemble and then manufacture bicycles in the United States.

Kamler has been through the usual challenges that beset anyone in business. In the past few years, he has renewed the company's commitment to quality manufacturing in the United States. Kent's new factory in Manning, South Carolina, Kamler's personal connection with his employees (whom he all knows by name), and new equipment to renew the process of bike-making that was nearly forgotten, all represent major reshoring work that is designed to rebuild the U.S. bike industry.

But as many manufacturers seeking to re-shore discover, you cannot rebuild a house if the foundation has been washed away. The machines are gone as tooling moved offshore along with manufacturing intelligence. Traditional manufacturing centers that trained the workforce died out.

Kamler got a commitment from state government that proved invaluable. He had expressed to the South Carolina Commerce Department that the company could not find a building with natural gas. The department arranged a personal phone call with Governor Nikki Haley. Even though his preferred location had none, the governor guaranteed that Kent's needs for energy, training, and physical requirements would be fulfilled and he came through on that promise.

Kamler is proud to bring production back to South Carolina. After moving its manufacturing overseas in 1990, because it proved to be less expensive, Kamler began reshoring after attending Walmart's Manufacturing Summit in August 2014.

Production in Manning began in the fall of 2014. When it is at full capacity in 2016, Kent expects to have added 175 jobs in assembly and parts production.

"It's exciting to see a leading manufacturer like Kent Bicycles choose South Carolina to manufacture bicycles, a mainstay of an American childhood," said Governor Haley. "We celebrate the company's decision to create at least 175 new jobs and produce a half a million bicycles annually in Clarendon County, and we are pleased that Walmart's commitment to domestic manufacturing is accelerating real progress on the issue."

Kent's plant in Manning started out assembling in-sourced parts, but the facility is beginning to produce more of its components, including forks, handlebars, rims, and frames, which are the most expensive components.

Production of frames and forks requires precise forming, welding, and finish work. There are 11 separate pieces that need to be welded into the frame, and they have to be precisely cut and machined to allow for robotic welding. Eleven welds are required to connect the frame components.

Because steel is not absolutely uniform—every batch has slight variations—each bike frame has to be carefully checked for alignment. After the frames are welded, they may need to be straightened out with a rubber mallet and precise alignment dies.

After the robot has completed frame welding and alignment, the frame moves to painting. Welding, cutting, bending, and painting are the biggest challenges they have. They are getting help from an unlikely source— their partners own a factory in China that is already doing robotic welding, and Kent is getting training and equipment from them.

As far as production process improvement is concerned, continuous improvement is an approach that is working at Kent. The factory workforce proposes and implements good improvements. The company looks at every single process. They have a team of six people, two of whom are engineers who have been in manufacturing for many years. The factory general manager is an engineer with great experience in robotic welding, power coating, and painting.

It is worthwhile to remember that while Kent is a big manufacturer that sells to Walmart, there are dozens of small handcraft bicycle makers in the United States that make everything from city cruisers to super expensive titanium racers. Among them is Bowery Lane Bicycles in Brooklyn, New York, owned and operated by family since 1891 and still hand making "bikes of yesterday but built for today."

A MERGER WITHOUT COMMITMENT: DAIMLERCHRYSLER

Commitment comes in many forms.

You can have a commitment to quality, a commitment to corporate responsibility, or a commitment to returning to your shareholders a fair profit.

Sometimes, you need a commitment to reality. This can be the most difficult of all!

On May 7, 1998, the auto world was stunned by the announcement of history's biggest cross-border union: German automaker Daimler-Benz AG was merging with Chrysler Corporation in a deal worth $38 billion. The conglomerate named, DaimlerChrysler AG, envisioned competing in all vehicle market divisions, manufacturing cars from $11,000 subcompacts to Mercedes sedans at $100,000.

"This is much more than a merger," said Jürgen Schrempp, the Daimler-Benz chairman who in January 1998 proposed the merger plan to Robert Eaton, Chrysler chairman and CEO. "Today we are creating the world's leading automotive company for the twenty-first century. We are combining the two most innovative car companies in the world."

The plan was intended to benefit both companies. For Chrysler, the deal provided entry to the European market, and in its manufacturing, Chrysler was to use Daimler components, parts, and vehicle architecture to reduce the cost of vehicle production. The merger provided Daimler-Benz a second line of cars and trucks at moderate prices, and opened expansion in the United States for the German auto giant.

The merger failed. Nine years later, in early 2007, Daimler sold 80 percent of Chrysler to private equity firm Cerberus Capital Management LLC for $7.4 billion. Daimler returned to its luxury Mercedes brand and its truck business, while the private equity firm in New York assured Chrysler it would regain its former status "to the first ranks of the U.S. and global auto industry."

As we now know, Chrysler is now a subsidiary of Fiat. By all accounts, the current marriage seems to be a happy one, in contrast to the previous union, which ended in an ugly divorce.

What happened with Daimler? According to Dave Healy, an analyst with Burnham Securities, "You had two companies from different countries with different languages and different styles come together yet there were no synergies. It was simply an exercise in empire-building by Jürgen Schrempp."

Somewhere along the line, there was no commitment to reality. It was just a very expensive fantasy.

The deal went sour and DaimlerChrysler gained control. Former Chrysler chairman Lee Iacocca commented, "[Chrysler Chairman and CEO] Bob Eaton panicked ... We were making $1 billion a quarter and had $12 billion in cash, and while he said it was a merger of equals, he sold Chrysler to Daimler-Benz, when we should have bought them."

Problems arose when the luxury division of Daimler's Mercedes-Benz went back on their word to share high-end components with Chrysler.

Meanwhile, Daimler underrated the competition that was invading the car market in North America and gaining domestic carmakers' market share.

Schrempp stated in 2000, "If I had gone and said Chrysler would be a division, everybody on their side would have said: 'There is no way we'll do a deal.' " Public response to his comments was anger, and a lawsuit was launched by Kirk Kerkorian, a former shareholder, and Daimler-Chrysler won.

Chrysler sales slipped, and in 2000 Daimler dispatched Dieter Zetsche to Detroit to turn Chrysler around. With Zetsche as CEO, Chrysler reported a $1.8 billion gain in 2005. But in 2006, Chrysler experienced a loss of $1.47 billion dollars from slumping sales of trucks and SUVs because of skyrocketing prices of fuel.

It is a verity of business that mergers and acquisitions designed to produce synergy between two companies often fail. The bright idea usually comes from the top because CEOs and senior managers see synergies and benefits that do not matter to consumers, and they fail to take seriously the differences in corporate culture.

It all comes down to commitment. If there is no commitment, a quickie divorce may soon follow.

PROFILE: TOM WYNN, PEERLESS CHAIN

My good friend Tom Wynn in Winona has executed a bite-sized acquisitions strategy really well. Tom's company, Peerless Chain, is literally right down the street from mine in Winona. It is a bedrock Midwestern manufacturer that has become an industry consolidator. Peerless makes heavy industrial chains, the big stuff that is used on machines like commercial fishing boats and cranes.

When Tom took over as president and CEO, the company was selling everything it made. Peerless was number four in its industry and had about 17 percent market share. It had just the one location in Winona. Tom could see the writing on the wall. Unless Peerless got bigger they would eventually be swallowed up in an acquisition or blown out by competitors who were growing. Sound familiar?

Tom and his executive crew kicked themselves into high gear. In nine years they bought and digested four companies. Peerless tripled the size of its top-line revenue and went from being number four in its sector to number one. As of 2014, it had 40 percent of the industrial chain market. Tom shared those numbers with me when I interviewed him that year to discuss his acquisition strategy.

"First of all, don't overpay," Tom cautions. Sounds simple enough, right? But a lot of companies do. If you are small-to-mid-sized like Peerless and Miller Ingenuity, your acquisitions will likely be—or *should* be—smaller, closely held companies. A lot of them are first or second-generation owned with niche products. One thing you must watch out for is that, "Privately held family-owned businesses usually overstate their worth," as Tom said. The owners have a lot of blood, sweat, and tears invested, and they want to cash in on that. Can you blame them? No! But you have to make them understand financial realities.

Tom told me about one family business he was eyeing in Florida with a $1 million EBITA, but they wanted $12 million. You cannot be paying multiples of 10 or 12. So, he walked away. I have walked away from some deals too because of price, or because the fit was not right.

Investing time in creating quality commitments will positively benefit your bottom line. Build a secure foundation for your business by making informed commitments, sharing your values and integrity, and ensuring you have the ability to provide your customers with your goods and services.

NINE

The Sixth Value of Ingenuity—Excellence

For all you hard-nosed business people who think you do not have time for the "soft" stuff of values, this chapter is for you! It is chock full of hard ideas, concepts, tools, and processes you can use to drive your business to heights that you never dreamed of.

But be forewarned: If you have not laid the groundwork with the first five Values of Ingenuity™, the tools and techniques in this chapter will be useless. It is okay if you skipped to this chapter to find out what the "hard" stuff is. Remember, though, that without the "soft" stuff there will be no "hard" stuff. So if you were tempted to skip to this chapter and just get the hard stuff going, don't do it, because I guarantee you will fail.

Often when I consult with CEOs they tell me their problem is they have no time to implement the soft stuff because they have an urgent need to fix the business, and they think focusing solely on excellence is the answer.

I understand. Just like them, many times I have been tempted to get the hard stuff going. I have been in business firefights where I have felt an over-whelming urgency to vastly improve the financials *right now*. And no doubt there may be times you will be under fire from your board or shareholders to do something dramatic, visible, and "hard" right now.

When the business is in dire straits, boards and shareholders want to see action. Even when they simply desire better performance, they will push you to be visible and dramatic. They will not want to hear about this "values stuff."

I once described to a board how I was implementing total quality (yes, it was that long ago) in the company and how I had engaged all of the employees to help design and implement the effort. Do you want to know the reaction I got from the board to that idea? "Oh, at our company we wouldn't *ask* people; we would just *do* it." Well, "just do it" may be a good slogan if you are selling athletic shoes, but it is not good for the rest of us.

This illustrates how all but the most enlightened boards will push you for action, not reflection. Wall Street likes action. Stock prices move when there is visible evidence of action. Capital is attracted to action. But when your business requires dramatic improvement, you need to begin with reflection, not action. "Don't just do something—stand there!" should be your motto. You may have only one shot at getting it right. If you launch into action for action's sake, it will confuse the organization. In the end it will be counterproductive at best and destructive at worst. Action can lead to reaction. Reaction then leads to more action, which then leads to. . . . You get the picture: a vicious cycle.

"But if my board is demanding action, I have to satisfy them," you say. Perhaps, but always remember this: If you let your board push you into action that you know to be wrong, and it turns out it was, they will not blame themselves. They will blame *you*. So you can take your hard knocks on the front end by resisting their calls for action, or you can get canned on the back end when things do not work out. It is really as simple as that.

So take the time to lay the groundwork with the other Values of Ingenuity™ before you tackle this one. Assuming you have done this, let's turn our attention to what the Ingenuity Value of Excellence really means.

DEFINING "EXCELLENCE"

Excellence is such an overused term it almost has no practical meaning in business anymore. Do you know of any companies that have a motto of "We're average," or "We're not so bad," or "We're not great but we're not horrible either"? Of course not. Most companies claim they are the best at what they do. Many companies make claims that they are excellent. Truth in advertising applies only if one can prove the claims otherwise. When a company makes a nebulous claim of being excellent, it cannot be disproved because it is not defined. That is because most companies that make this claim do not even know what it means themselves.

What does it mean to their employees? What standards of performance are they supposed to strive for to be "excellent"? Since companies do not know the answer to what it means for the company, they leave it vague and expect employees to figure out what "excellent" really means. After all, they went to high school, didn't they? Doesn't everyone know what "excellent" means?

And just to show they are serious about this excellent stuff, companies will include an area in performance appraisals to rate employees on how excellent they are. And worse yet, they chastise employees for not being excellent when they have not even defined what it means!

No wonder many employees feel the so-called value of excellence is just a joke.

When CEOs ask me to help them on the path to excellence, I start with some diagnostics and some questions to determine whether they really need to, or want to, be excellent at all. Take the time right now to answer these questions for your organization:

What does excellence mean to you, your customers and employees? Your standard of excellence and mine are probably completely different. Your standard of excellence and those of your customers, suppliers, and employees are also probably different. At the end of the day, the only standard that counts is the one dictated by the customer. Do you know what that standard is? Have you talked to your customers to find out if they want excellence—and just as importantly, are they willing to pay for it?

"But don't all customers want excellence?" you say. Hardly. Do you expect excellence in a snow shovel? What about in an artificial heart machine? You would expect the shovel to be functional but the artificial heart machine to be excellent, wouldn't you?

Do you expect excellence in your wireless cell phone provider? How about in your satellite television provider? Okay, maybe the last one was a trick question. Nobody expects excellence in cell phone and satellite television providers. And why is that? Simple: Everyone knows they cannot have it. In the case of the satellite providers, you have only two choices, so they can do whatever they want. For either of them to go to the expense of becoming "excellent" would be silly and unnecessary.

And it is entirely possible that the value of excellence is totally unnecessary in your business. The worst thing you could do is implement excellence for excellence's sake.

And always remember that what customers *want* and what they are willing to *pay for* are often two different things. In many industries customers want excellent quality, delivery, and customer service, but only as long as they do not have to pay extra for it. Sound unfair? Probably, but it is the world of today. But since you will not get paid extra for excellence, be sure you understand your customer's definition so you are not over-delivering on excellence because that would just add cost without a profit offset.

What Does "Excellence" Mean to Your Organization or Business?

Knowing what the customer expects will not give you the answer to this question. Often customers have only a vague idea, if they have any idea at all, of what their expectations for standards of performance are. Sure, they will tell you they want a good price, delivery, and quality. But what does that mean? Does that mean the lowest price of any competitor? Does that mean delivery immediately, tomorrow, next month, or next year? Does quality mean zero defects, an occasional defect, or an extended warranty? You need to answer these questions precisely before you can implement standards of excellence in your organization to meet those customer expectations.

THE COST OF EXCELLENCE

What would it cost your organization to become excellent?

If you have defined what the customer requires, and you have determined that it will require excellence in your organization to satisfy them, then the next question becomes this: Can you afford it? Do not just go into an excellence campaign without knowing with complete clarity the cost to the organization, not only in money but in employee churn, as an initiative of this type will require you to replace many existing employees. As you will read in this chapter, implementing excellence can be a very costly undertaking, so you better know what you are getting into before you get started. As in all corporate initiatives, you do not want to start unless you can go the distance.

Do You Know Exactly What You Would Gain by Becoming Excellent?

You need to do a careful cost-benefit analysis to determine the likely yield from such a program. Will you be able to increase price and improve margin? Will you be able to gain share from a competitor? Will you be able to enter markets that were closed to you before? Make sure you involve your finance people and get hard, verifiable, credible numbers on this. In programs like this, the cost is always certain, but the payoff can often be a pipe dream, so be sure the payoff is there.

And what if it is not? What if the analysis points out no gains? Then don't do it.

Why go through all that trouble and expense just to hang a banner on the wall or brag to your customers about how excellent you are?

Be very deliberate in making that decision. Table stakes change all the time in business, and while it may not be necessary to be excellent today, it probably will be necessary tomorrow.

As you will learn in this chapter, achieving excellence requires these steps:

1. Precisely define it.
2. Strictly adhere to it.
3. Continuously reinforce, recognize, and reward it.

Excellence Is an Internal Value

Do not make the mistake of hanging a banner on a wall and declaring the organization is now magically excellent. Do not make the mistake of striving for excellence if the business does not need it or cannot afford it. And finally, do not make the mistake of bragging to the outside world that you are excellent. No one will believe you anyway. Excellence is an internal value, not an external badge of honor. Excellence is an internal operating philosophy, not an advertising tool. Let your advertising tool be the standards of performance you bring to the customer that no one else can.

LEAN PRODUCTION IN ACTION

All across America, there are profitable manufacturers who are doing amazing things, and we are grateful to learn many lessons from them. In this book, I have included just a few of their stories, and they reveal the diversity of solutions and approaches taken by successful businesses.

But since excellence is such a highly subjective value that each enterprise needs to figure out for itself, I thought the best way to tackle the subject would be to tell you how I have implemented lean production in some of the companies I have led. I hope that you will be able to take away valuable insights that will help your company define and achieve excellence.

Here is how I have introduced and have maintained a lean approach.

1. Educate! When implementing a new program, it is always important to get everyone to the same level of understanding so they can be active participants. Hands-on training, where the employees are actively engaged, is always the most effective. Demystify it for everyone because they will reject what they do not understand. This is where you present the target for everyone to see and show them the path to get there. Break it down into bite-size pieces that are easy to digest.

It is okay to have people challenge the new program. You want to embrace their skepticism and make them believers. After the program has been implemented, they will be your strongest supporters.

Whenever I have implemented lean manufacturing, I had all employees participate in a full day introductory training session. I brought in an outside consultant who had experience implementing lean in various facilities and was capable of answering all employee questions with meaningful and honest answers.

The focus of the training is always role-playing a factory setting, and we start by using Lego to build airplanes. Imagine that for creative training!

The first session uses traditional methods for building the planes. Then after each session, we would do a debrief to discuss what went well and what not so well. Then we learned some lean techniques and devised a plan to utilize them in the following session. We repeated this process several times throughout the day. Each time, the participants saw for themselves that the lean techniques they had learned and utilized resulted in a better process. By the end of the day, everyone had experienced a complete lean transformation.

2. Choose the operational area. After getting everyone on board with the program, the next step is to identify an area to implement what was learned in the training. Some companies have tried to run multiple kaizen events at the same time right out of the gate. I believe you have a greater chance of success if you pick one area to start with and do it well. Make it the model for others to replicate. Celebrate the small victories. Keep it visible for everyone to see. Allow others to come over to observe and ask questions. Use participants from the first kaizen event to help with kaizen events in other areas. It is important to do this immediately after the training to keep the momentum going. We would always have an area picked out knowing that if we could implement lean there, we could implement it anywhere.

3. Map the value stream. This is the analysis method of all the events that occur from beginning to end of producing a product or service to customer delivery. Toyota named it "material and information flow mapping."

The value stream mapping team should include manufacturing employees from the area, as well as engineering support. To achieve buy-in from the start, it is important to have the manufacturing employees from the area involved in the process. If they are not part of the process change, they will not sustain the process change you are trying to implement. Start with the current state and identify all of the steps in the manufacturing process. Detail is very important so you do not miss any of the steps regardless of how insignificant they may seem. Videotaping the manufacturing process in action is a great way to do it, as you can replay all of the steps and use a time stamp to calculate the time for each step. It is also imperative to create a spaghetti diagram that shows the flow of product, people, and paper throughout the manufacturing process. This needs to be the *actual* flow, not the *perceived* flow, as we are looking to document any unnecessary motion.

Based on your current demand, you would then determine the necessary *takt* time for manufacturing to keep up with demand. (*Takt* time, derived from the German word *Taktzeit*, translated best as "meter," is the average unit production time needed to meet customer demand.)

Once this is complete, then you move on to creating the value stream map for the area in the future state utilizing the concepts learned in the lean training. It is here that you determine what steps in the process add value to your customer and then take action to remove waste (transportation, inventory, motion, waiting, over-processing, over-production, defects, and under-utilized talent) wherever possible. For each process step ask if it adds value to the product or if it is required (certifications or regulations) by the customer. If neither, then eliminate that step. You should strive for one-piece continuous flow.

4. Marshal your equipment, tools, and inventory. Once the future state value stream map is complete, then look at your equipment and decide what can be used as is and what needs to be modified or replaced. Remember that lean is not about purchasing brand new equipment. Instead, look for opportunities to use existing equipment whenever possible. It is important that this equipment be reliable. You cannot afford to have regular outages of the equipment.

Then create 2-D models of the equipment and move them around on a floor map of the area to look at different manufacturing cell configurations that can give you the one-piece continuous flow you are striving for in the future state value stream map. Analyze each layout for pros and cons to facilitate comparison of the various layouts. Do not be constrained by current walls, electrical, plumbing and so forth. If, in fact, the best configuration requires changes to infrastructure, it may be worth the investment to do so.

It may be necessary to replace current equipment if it is suited only for batch type manufacturing and does not support one-piece flow. Start by looking for off-the-shelf solutions but be ready to come up with a custom design if necessary. Get the team involved in generating ideas for this new design. Look for ways to prototype the equipment and trying it out before designing and building the final version.

Here is a perfect example of a process that was changed using lean principles. One of the steps in a process was soaking parts in oil for a period of time. This was achieved with a batch approach—we stacked multiple parts into a large basket and then dipped the basket into a tank. When going to one-piece flow, the team came up with a Ferris wheel concept. Although we were fairly confident it would work, it was expensive to build and had a long lead time. In order to test out the theory, we instead purchased rectangular flower pots, the first filled with oil and the second left empty for the parts to drain. We incorporated the flower pots into the process and the operators pushed the parts through them to simulate the same dipping and draining time they would see on the Ferris wheel. Not only did this prove the concept, but allowed us to move forward with our kaizen event and start manufacturing in our new cells.

Prior to starting the kaizen event, determine how much time it will take to make the transformation including hiccups, startup time, and getting comfortable with the new lean process. Then you can determine how much finished product inventory will be required to cover you for that period of time, and you can proceed to build this inventory. You should also get contractors lined up for the time period you have scheduled for the kaizen event. This included plumbing, electrical, rigging—whatever is required to move the equipment around during the kaizen event. It was important to have them on-site during the event to minimize any delays during the transformation.

5. Hold the kaizen event. Once you have decided the layout, hold pre-planning meetings with the entire team including contractors. You want to ensure that everyone is on the same page to ensure a timely and safe transformation of the area.

When you get to the day of the event, start with a quick meeting in the morning to review the plan for the day and make sure you have everything required to do the job. At the end of the day, get together again to update everyone on the status and make any changes to the plan for the next day. Communication is the key throughout the process. You can never over-communicate.

The last part of the kaizen event is to do a safety review to make sure that you have not introduced any new safety hazards into the area as a result of the changes made or new equipment added. Address any issues immediately with the same vigor that the transformation was carried out. A safety incident would put a damper on what should be a very exciting event.

6. Take it for a test drive. Once the kaizen event is complete and the new layout has been realized, it is time to give it a try. Again, you want to do this as soon as possible, with the excitement level high after completing the transformation.

Start with a plan as to what you want to try out. Begin with a quick meeting to get everyone on the same page. Set the expectation that output is not important at this point. Emphasis should be placed on learning the new process and staying true to the one-piece flow concept learned in the lean training. As before, safety is of the utmost importance, along with meeting any quality requirements. It is important to have support personnel (engineering, maintenance, etc.) available during the start-up to resolve any issues that come up. It should be their number one priority. At the end of each day, get the team together to discuss what went well and what they would like to change. Be careful not to change things too hastily as it may be part of the learning curve.

Always document the current process and times before making changes to the process. Develop an action plan for the changes you would like to make, implement the changes, and check to see if they have the desired effect. If not, go back to your previous state. As the team becomes more comfortable with the process, then challenge them to increase the output. Determine what a reasonable output is and set that as the target for the team to benchmark themselves against. Once you have the process working as desired, it is important to document what you have and also to review any quality procedures or work instructions to see if they need to be updated to support the new process.

7. Celebrate! Last, but not least, celebrate the victory. Thank everyone for their participation and maintain the excitement level for moving forward with other projects.

The team should strive for continuous improvement. Lean is a journey, not a destination. The team should always look for new ideas to address problem areas or constraints in their process. More often than not, the best time to discover these opportunities is when a new employee is brought into the area. They are more likely to ask the questions as to why something is being done in a certain way, which may spark a brainstorming session and generate new ideas.

While the excitement level is high, identify the next area in which you would like to undertake a lean transformation via a kaizen event. Identify team members from the area to take on the project. More likely than not, you will have more volunteers than you need because of the excitement generated from the previous project. Also recruit one or two star team members from the previous project. They will be the best promoters of the change you are looking to make and will be able to dispel any of the concerns that may arise, as they most likely had similar concerns before starting their event.

THE 5S METHODOLOGY

If you do nothing else with lean, at the very least implement the 5S methodology: sort, straighten, shine, standardize, and sustain. It is imperative for the employees to be part of this process if you want them to internalize it.

1. Sort. Go through everything in your area and remove anything that is not needed. The key word is *needed*. Some people will struggle with this, especially if they have saved everything from day one. Some items are easy to get rid of while others may be more difficult as there may be a need to use something occasionally or nobody is sure what it is used for. The latter should be put in a quarantine area until the team is comfortable that they are no longer needed. A notable example is a wrench set. If only a few of the wrenches are required, get the remaining wrenches out of the area.

2. Straighten. Organize the remaining items so they are easily accessible and in the right area to do the job. If the same wrench is required for two different operations that are out of reach of each other, it will be to your benefit to purchase a second wrench, placing one each next to the operation required. One technique is to utilize shadow boards for storing tools. This assures that every tool has a place and it is easy to identify when a tool is missing. Tools should be labeled for their purpose. Color coding can also be used to your advantage to differentiate areas or operations.

3. Shine. Cleaning the area has many benefits, with safety being most important. Remove clutter and tripping hazards, and clean up spills, especially oil and grease that can be slipping hazards. Ensure that items stored on shelves will not fall down. The second benefit is improved efficiency. Not having to work around or move clutter, and not having to find the right tool covered by a heap of other tools will save time. Last but not least, is the sense of pride that employees have for their work area when it is cleaned.

4. Standardize. To ensure consistency in the process, it is important that everyone does everything the same way (standard work). The first step is to identify what is the best practice for each process step. Once that is established, this needs to be documented in a work instruction. Make work instructions as visual as possible. Post them on the line where the operations are taking place. Work instructions that are nothing but pages of boring text will never get read. Look to employ video whenever possible. Also consider going electronic with your work instructions and using tablets on the manufacturing floor. Whenever possible, try to standardize across different work areas, which will make it easier for employees to flex from one area to another when demand requires you to shift resources.

5. Sustain. This is the heart of the 5S methodology and the reason most 5S implementations fail. If you are unable to sustain it, then you have wasted your time with the other elements.

Your employees need to see the benefits of doing 5S and buy into it. If not, they will not internalize it. This requires constant vigilance at the beginning, and I found it better to recognize and reward those areas that were doing a good job versus scolding and penalizing those areas that were not doing a good job. 5S is everyone's job and needs to be part of the performance expectations. It is equally important to allot time during the regular workday to do this.

Take the last 15 minutes each day for 5S. It is that important.

Wherever possible, take advantage of vendor-managed inventory. Utilize it for all of your hardware that is used in your assemblies as well as MRO supplies. Have *kanbans* set up in your area supermarkets and only stock to those levels. (*Kanban*, which means "signboard" or "billboard" in Japanese, is a scheduling system for lean and just-in-time production.) Your vendor should come in daily to replenish your supermarkets and invoice only for that amount. Issue blanket purchase orders for your annual requirements and receive the daily replenishments against that. The benefits are no stock outs, significantly reduced inventory levels, and reduced number of POs generated.

Strive for strategic partnerships with your suppliers and understand that it is the *total* cost of doing business and not just the *part* cost that is important. With that in mind, you should work with your suppliers to minimize the number of times you are handling their product. That includes the quantity packaged per container, the type of container, and how often it is delivered. Whenever possible, try to match the quantity packaged with the quantity typically ordered so that in most cases you are able to ship the package directly without having to repack it. In the case of materials used in manufacturing areas, try to have the container size match the supermarket space available for it. As for deliveries, have several of your high volume materials delivered on a weekly or biweekly basis. Most, if not all raw materials should be visible on the manufacturing floor.

Incorporate *poka-yoke* (mistake proofing) into your processes. The more you do this, the more intuitive the process and the less likely that mistakes will be made. A secondary benefit is that fewer work instructions are required to document the process.

For example, you should have several assembly/weld/machining fixtures that only allow you to put the part in one way. If you try to insert it any other way, it just does not fit.

This also facilitates flexing of employees from one area to another when demand requires you to shift resources.

SINGLE MINUTE EXCHANGE OF DIES (SMED)

With the trend toward make-to-order and smaller run sizes, the need to implement single minute exchange of dies (SMED) is imperative. I liken this to the pit crews of NASCAR as they refuel and change tires. If the car is not on the track, you are not winning races. Likewise, if your machine is not making parts, you are not making money. The goal is to make tooling change-outs as quickly as possible. Look for ways to standardize across tooling so you are using common parts and methods. Utilize standardized frames with replaceable inserts whenever possible. Utilize quick release functionality whenever feasible to minimize the number of tools required for the job. Keep asking yourself what can be done to the tooling to make it easier and quicker to change out.

On the surface, some ideas may seem wild and expensive. When you dig into the numbers and calculate the savings created over the life of the project, the changes you are considering will often pay for themselves several times over.

It is all too common for prototype tooling to turn into production tooling because you are squeezed for time. Prototype tooling allows you to get samples parts out in the shortest lead time and lowest cost. This usually comes at the expense of setup time, cycle time, and ease of use. Go back and build the production tooling you intended in the first place and incorporate SMED concepts wherever possible. You will realize the savings and improve the morale of the employees who have to work with it.

Most factories have only one or two setup people for a particular area. This makes it difficult to accomplish quick tooling changeovers, especially if you have multiple tools that need to be changed at the same time.

In the self-directed work team methodology, you want as many employees as possible with the capability to change out tooling. This facilitates the pit crew mentality. Get in. Change the tool. Get out. Start making parts.

PERFORMANCE METRICS REALIZED BY IMPLEMENTING LEAN

Here are some actual performance metrics realized by implementing lean. The bullet points are aggregated from several companies that I have led.

Inventory

- Inventory reduction of 20–50 percent.
- Vendor-managed inventory for sourced parts (hardware stocked daily).
- Minimal work in process inventory.
- Significantly reduced subassembly or finished-product inventory.
- Significantly reduced levels of piece part and raw material inventory.

Production

- Transformed from "make to stock" to "make to order."
- Dramatic lead time reduction.
- Line changeover time reduced significantly.
- Labor reduction of up to 50 percent.
- Increase in available factory space equivalent to adding another shift.

SELF-DIRECTED WORK TEAMS

The self-directed work team methodology is based on a simple premise: Expect more from your employees and you will get more. The goal is to have everyone actively engaged and contributing to the success of the business. Actively recruit people who have the right attitude and give them the tools they need to thrive in a self-directed work team environment.

Your manufacturing employees should work together, without the usual managerial supervision, to ensure that customer orders are manufactured to specification and shipped on time. Every day should start with a debrief meeting where employees should discuss safety concerns, quality concerns, and the production schedule. They should also decide if resources are needed elsewhere and flex accordingly as all are cross-trained to work in all areas.

In order to achieve that, you will need to implement a behavior-based pay system, a performance-based bonus, and an employee referral program.

The behavior-based pay system starts with establishing the various levels you want for the workforce. The fewer the levels the better. Keep it simple. You should not need more than three levels:

Operator I (entry level with no experience)
Operator II (usually a referral with experience)
Operator specialist (leaders)

Peer reviews, based on an expectation matrix, should be conducted on a regular basis and provide feedback for advancement. An operator specialist is not a supervisor. They are a "super team member" who continue to do the same tasks that are expected of an operator I and operator II. The difference is that they exhibit leadership behaviors that are conducive to building a strong and coherent team. Your goal is to have all operator specialists (inverted pyramid). This results in fewer safety incidents, fewer quality issues, less turnover, less training, less supervision, and more flexibility.

What is unique about this structure is that each of the levels has a set wage and days of vacation. It is *not* based on seniority or years of service. Remember, your customers do not care how long you have been around. There should be a significant pay differential between operator I and operator II, of at least $3 per hour, and between operator II and operator specialist of $5 per hour. This encourages people to strive for the operator specialist level. Likewise, vacation should be set at one week for operator I, two weeks for operator II, and three weeks for operator specialist. More important, there are no "time in grade" requirements for moving to the next level. The only requirement for advancement is that the employee's peers agree that the employee exhibits and sustains the behaviors spelled out in the expectation matrix for the next level.

Once you have the levels established, then you need to construct the expectation matrix. Assemble a team from all functional areas to determine the critical behaviors you want your operators to exhibit at the various levels. The critical behaviors document is not intended to list every possible behavior (like a rule book or checklist); more so it is intended to be a guideline. Interestingly enough, people who are good candidates for self-directed work teams will feel comfortable with the expectation matrix because it paves a path without being overbearing. On the other hand, people who are not good candidates for self-directed work teams will struggle with the expectation matrix, because it is not structured or detailed enough for them.

Peer Review

The most important part of the self-directed work team methodology is the peer review process. This starts with a self-review where each employee reviews their performance against the expectation matrix and records this in the first column of the evaluation sheet. Then the employees get together, usually in their functional teams. The process starts with one of the employees presenting their self-review to their team members. Then the team members, one by one, give their feedback to the employee and the employee records this in the second column of the evaluation sheet. After all team members have given their feedback, then the employee comes up with an action plan to address the opportunities for improvement and records this in the third column of the evaluation sheet. These are the areas that the employee will work on over the next several months. This becomes the starting point for the follow-up peer review session with the employee starting the process all over with a self-review of the items listed on the action plan.

The operator specialist level is not on a pedestal nor is it untouchable. They have to continue to perform and improve themselves daily. Operator specialists should hold peer reviews amongst themselves to ensure that everyone is performing at a level befitting of the position.

The peer review process is carried out more frequently for new employees (weekly) and becomes less frequent (monthly) as they progress. Put an emphasis on new employee development to give them the best probability of success and utilize "on the job" training as the primary method for knowledge sharing. If it is evident that a new employee is not a good fit for the self-directed work team environment, waste no time in parting ways. Everybody goes through the evaluation process at least twice a year. One of the points to stress is that feedback is always most effective when given as close in time to the actual event as possible. This way the employee has the best recollection of the event and is able to effectively apply the feedback. The preference is to give this feedback immediately and not wait until the next scheduled peer review session.

As it is difficult and uncomfortable for many people to give constructive feedback to someone else, the majority of the coaching for self-directed work teams has to be focused on this aspect. Peer reviews should bring constructive criticism with the intent of building team members up, not putting them down. Starting out, most employees will want to bring up only the positive points. I refer to this as the "powder puff" phase. Most employees are feeling out the process and have some fear of retaliation from their teammates. What you should coach is that the feedback has to be "real" to be effective. As with the lean training, role playing is the best way to teach the peer review process. The feedback has to strike a balance of reinforcing the areas where the employee is doing well and pointing out areas that need improvement. That is the only way the team will get better.

One of the most important rules of peer reviews is to be respectful of each other—that is, no mudslinging. As the person receiving feedback, it is important to listen, and that means really listen. Ask clarifying questions, if necessary, but never lash back or refute what the other person is saying.

As the person giving the feedback, focus on the behavior, not the person. Provide detail, bringing up examples whenever possible. Realize that the person may not even be aware they are doing what you say or that their actions are being perceived in the manner in which they are.

Bonuses Based on the Profit Target

Everyone should have the opportunity to earn an annual bonus based on one performance target, the only one that matters—profit. This single metric is easy to understand and assures that all employees are pulling in the same direction. The bonus scale should be a significant percentage of base salary that scales up for attaining 100 percent, 105 percent, and 110 percent of company profit budget. Performance against this target needs to be shared monthly. The job of your leaders is to coach employees on how they can positively impact the profit of the company.

You would be amazed that if you implement this system, when profit falls below the target, employees will come to you to see if there are additional things they can do in or out of their areas to bring it back above target. Here is a great example of this in action. Once, some employees brought it to my attention that the customary practice of working overtime the last week of the month was negatively affecting profit and ultimately their bonuses. They wanted to smooth production so the overtime was not necessary. How many companies do you know where the employees will challenge overtime opportunities, in which they are guaranteed to make extra money in the short term, to help the company achieve its long-term goals?

When recruiting new employees, strive to get as many employee referrals as possible. People typically associate with others who have similar mindsets, and this mindset is telltale of their ability to thrive in a self-directed work team environment. To incentivize this process, offer a $500 bonus if the person referred is still employed after the first year and an additional $1,000 bonus if the person referred is still employed after the second year. It might seem like employees would take advantage of the system and refer anybody they know that is looking for job. On the contrary, employees are very protective of their reputations and do not refer others whom they feel would tarnish them.

All employees will know which new employees are referrals and who referred them. Through the peer review process, they have the opportunity to weed out any bad actors long before anyone receives a referral bonus. Operator specialists are involved in the interview process and decide whether or not they want to bring someone on board.

It is important to know before you start your journey into self-directed work teams that not everyone will make the trip. Some may not be comfortable with the self-directed work team environment or comfortable with change in general. Others may not be willing to exert the effort needed or just do not like what they are doing. And still others may not be capable of working in a team or in a self-directed environment. When you implement self-directed work teams, it is likely that you could have turnover as much as 50 percent. This will not happen all at once, nor do you want it to. It will be spread out over several years as it becomes self-evident that these individuals are not a fit. Some will leave on their own accord, while others will need to be asked to leave. An important distinction that needs to be understood is that many of these will be good people who are just not a good fit for the self-directed work team environment.

The most difficult decisions will be your best performers from the old system. They are individual contributors who excel at what they do. The downside is that they do not fit in a self-directed work team environment because they are not willing to put the success of the team above their individual success. They keep information to themselves to maintain an edge over their peers. They do not communicate or play well with others. They do not go out of their way to help others. When you let these individuals go, you will lose productivity in the short term, but will quickly gain it back as the team becomes stronger.

TEN

The Seventh Value of Ingenuity—Innovation

It is an axiom in business that the only thing that is constant is change. If you do not change, you will go out of business.

What does this mean, exactly? Does it apply to every facet of your business? Should you attempt to change everything all the time?

The answer is, "yes and no."

First, I will discuss the "no."

In any business venture, some things must *never* change or be compromised. The things that never change are your bedrock values. The 7 Values of Ingenuity™—Respect, Integrity, Teamwork, Community, Commitment, Excellence, and Innovation—must always stay in place, like the Rock of Gibraltar! Respect is the same thing today as it was a century ago, and it will be the same a century from now. Likewise, for integrity, teamwork, and the others. They have been the same since the dawn of time, and have been proven to be immutable. Disregard them at your peril.

This means that you must never abandon any of The 7 Values of Ingenuity™ to chase what appears to be a short-term opportunity or as a way to get a jump on the competition. Remember the "Made in China 2025" plan? You need to think the same way. Think about your company one year, five years, ten years from now. Build a strong foundation that will support you through the challenges of intense competition and sudden economic downturns. (The question is not "if" there will be another recession, but "when." Economies run in cycles. They go up and down. Always have, always will.)

So what should you always seek to change—that is, improve?

The answer is that you need to constantly do two things:

1. Know what your customers want, and provide it to them.
2. Do this in such a way that the company makes a profit.

The first qualification seems obvious. If your customers want a smartphone that tells them if there is a traffic jam up ahead on the highway, you'd better figure out how to give it to them, because your competitor is doing the same thing. If your smartphone 1.0 did not have traffic alerts, your smartphone 2.0 better have them. If not, your customers will seek satisfaction elsewhere, and you will soon go out of business.

The second qualification—to make a profit—is just as important as the first. The landscape of American manufacturing is littered with the empty carcasses of companies that offered fabulously innovative products but that failed to become profitable. They could not make money, and they went out of business.

Since we are talking about products, you might think that innovation, which is the seventh Value of Ingenuity™, refers primarily to the products you manufacture. In other words, if you make widget 1.0, then your widget 2.0 must be an improvement over its predecessor.

Yes, this is true. We live in a world of fast-paced technological advances, and consumers expect better and better products. The products that you make must always come as close as possible to perfectly satisfying your customer's expectations; and since these expectations change, you need to keep pace. Your widget 2.0 must be better at satisfying your customer than widget 1.0.

INNOVATION MUST TOUCH EVERY ASPECT OF YOUR COMPANY

I can hear the question now: "What if I'm in a business in which product change is unwelcome?"

Let's say you manufacture flour for baking. Your customers want Grandma's Flour to be exactly the same flour, with exactly the same characteristics, as the flour their grandma used. They do not want the slightest deviation. They do not want the product to reflect any form of innovation. They want every bag of flour to be exactly like the bag they bought last week, last year, and in the last century.

Okay, I can understand that. That is why the second qualification—to make a profit—is so important.

Innovation does not refer only to the product that your customers pick off the shelf. It refers to *every aspect of the process used to make your product*. Innovation should touch every stage of production and every corner of your business. Without affecting the product itself, you can innovate how you manufacture your product. You can innovate in your human resources policies. You can innovate how you share profits with your employees. You can innovate how you acquire energy for your factory.

Every innovation you make behind the scenes will impact your ability to satisfy your customer and make a profit.

For example, let's look at the example of Grandma's Flour.

The goal, in this case, is to make flour that is identical to the flour grandma used 50 years ago. I know there are thousands of different varieties of flour, but we will imagine that Grandma's Flour is a product with distinctive characteristics—it is made from a certain type of wheat, with a particular protein content and moisture content, and so on. Grandma's customers expect each bag of Grandma's Flour to be identical to the one before it.

By the way, if Grandma wants to introduce an entirely new variety of flour, this innovation (which may be a very good idea) needs to be given a separate label, like Grandma's Special Winter Wheat Formula. It would then be a product innovation acceptable to Grandma's customers.

Back to the basic flour product. Let's say that a foreign competitor starts selling flour in Grandma's market. This foreign competitor pays its workers peanuts and has no regard for human rights, and consequently can undercut Grandma's on its wholesale price.

So then how can Grandma's Flour innovate and keep its market share with its ubiquitous product?

There are countless ways to innovate that the customer never sees! The right innovations can lower production costs, cut waste in the manufacturing process, speed time to delivery, reduce rejects or bad product batches—the list goes on.

The idea is that while innovation refers to the product that your customer picks off the shelf, it is just as important to remember that innovation is important to every aspect of your business—including the behind-the-scenes work the customer never sees.

Here are some of the key ways that you can drive innovation in your company.

Lead by Example

It is imperative that CEOs, and the entire executive team, openly show support for innovation. When employees witness unanimous encouragement to participate in creative activities, it will strengthen and cultivate a team that is more receptive to creativity and innovative ideas.

Encourage New Ideas

When you have a community of people who are capable of creative, out-of-the-box thinking, you need to give them an environment where innovation is encouraged, managed, and rewarded.

Get everyone involved in a team culture that allows them to express their perspectives and new innovative ideas. Define their positions around innovation.

In 1948, 3M gave their professionals the opportunity to work on projects of their choosing for 15 percent of their time. Imagine how it was received at a time when executives in postwar America were donning grey flannel suits and going to offices with rigid hierarchies! But for 3M, it was a logical next step. From its early years as a struggling company, 3M learned they must "innovate or die." Once a year 3M employees display their special projects looking like they are presenting dinosaur models at their sixth-grade science fair. After putting up their poster, they stand next to it, looking for suggestions, feedback, and potential co-collaborators.

Every person working at any job in America should have the same opportunity. We should never lose our sense of childlike wonder and desire to dream up wacky ideas. I know from personal experience that you cannot get that one good idea without gratefully receiving the other 99 crazy ideas. Human beings are creatures of emotion. Too often a worker has an idea, but he or she gets scared that the boss will laugh at them or dismiss them. Their idea is fragile and vulnerable, like a tiny flower. So to keep from getting stomped on, they keep their little idea to themselves—and the company loses.

Unfettered creativity can sometimes pay off in spectacular fashion. In 1974, 3M scientist Art Fry came up with a little invention. By applying an adhesive (formulated by colleague Spencer Silver several years earlier) to the back of a slip of paper, he created a nifty bookmark that kept his place in his church hymnal. That is all he wanted to do—just keep his place in his hymnal at church. He called his gizmo the Post-It Note.

The best talent today expects flexibility from high-tech companies. You never know when one of these self-designed projects results in the next "must-have" product or even a whole new business.

Support Innovation

Make your company's dedication to innovation more than just a slogan on a poster, or a once-a-year brainstorming session with the boss ending it by saying, "Thanks, folks, for your ideas. Now get back to work." Transform the good new ideas into *action*. When a valuable idea is discovered and you want to give it a try, quickly allocate resources to develop the idea.

Do not waste time running ideas through numerous departments for feedback and approval. Rather, have an experienced small business determine quickly if you have a viable idea worth launching. Acting quickly will set your company apart as an innovator, and force your competition to up their game. For a small company, it is more feasible to delegate substantial resources quickly to work on the new idea. Reallocating sufficient resources in larger companies is more complex and will take longer if they have many product lines.

Listen to Your Customers

This is another one of those "no-brainer" concepts that, astonishingly, is too often ignored. Do not look at your customers as a source of annoying complaints; they are your best connection to reality!

Listen carefully to your customers' requests about improving your product or service. Then select which improvements will give you a return on your investment.

Customer complaints or difficulties with your products should be tracked and taken seriously, as they offer the opportunity for innovation.

Having said that, I am going to add two very important qualifiers.

A. Do not just ask your customers what they want; closely observe them and their behavior. Sometimes customers—especially those in the consumer sector—cannot articulate what they want because they do not know exactly what it is. Try to see how customers use your products. Do they use them in unexpected ways?

Heinz redesigned their ketchup bottles after noticing that customers preferred to store them upside down.

Levi Strauss saw that their customers intentionally ripped their jeans. Who would have thought that people wanted jeans with holes in them? They do, and so Levi's developed a line of pre-ripped jeans.

B. Sometimes you need to be one step ahead of your customer. "It's not the consumers' job to know what they want," Steve Jobs famously said. Jobs was speaking about products that no one had ever imagined but which, when consumers saw them, became hugely popular.

If product innovation is your main objective, should you ignore customer feedback? Is it possible for customers to understand what they want from successful businesses that are constantly pushing the boundaries in innovation?

There is a fine balance for innovative companies to decide how much customer feedback should influence their direction. By listening only to your customers or tracking current trends, you may end up walking at the tail end of the parade.

I will conclude with another famous quote. This one is from Henry Ford, who said, "If I had asked people what they wanted, they would have said, 'Faster horses.' "

Try Open Innovation

The central idea behind open innovation is that in a world with a wide variety of knowledge sources, businesses should seek external innovation sources and not solely trust their own findings. Some alternative methods include purchasing or licensing another company's invention, engaging in submissions competitions or participating in events that provide inexpensive access to a magnitude of innovative concepts.

As Alpheus Bingham and Dwayne Spradlin wrote in their book *The Open Innovation Marketplace*, an example of a small business leveraging challenges was Precyse Technologies. They specialize in (RFID) technology (radio frequency identification) data that is transferred wirelessly through electromagnetic fields to identify and track automatically, very small tags to objects. The tiny tags—each is not much larger than a grain of rice—contain information that is stored electronically; some powered from magnetic fields near the reader, by electromagnetic induction; and others are powered by battery far from the reader.

The company decided to hold a public competition to get new ideas by posting a global challenge to InnoCentive.com. Within three months, Precyse received more than two dozen legitimate submissions, several of which offered solutions that were both innovative and practical. The breakthrough winning result was—gathering energy from radio waves—that proved to significantly prolong the battery life of Precyse's RFID tags.

This innovation competition by Precyse empowered them to reach the market faster, with a higher quality product at lower costs, in an extremely competitive market.

Like any other methodology, open innovation is not going to work if you simply try to attach it to existing practices and processes. Many companies make a half-hearted effort and are surprised when they get mediocre outcomes as a result. Or they approach open innovation only shortsightedly, not realizing the enormous positive possibilities.

Open innovation not only offers limitless opportunities for resolving significant challenges and problems, but promotes and increases brand awareness as well.

Measure Innovation

For some reason, innovation is not considered by many companies when doing employee evaluations. Clearly identifying innovation in job descriptions motivates people to concentrate on creativity. Employees typically put their efforts only into activities specifically listed in their job descriptions. Emphasize innovation and the value of creative thinking to your entire workforce.

Challenge and encourage your workers who are close to the action, to uncover new work strategies and ways to enhance customer relations.

Your business plan should incorporate objectives for innovative products and services. Write innovation into everyone's objectives. Put it onto the balanced scorecard. Measure it and it will happen.

PROFILE: STEVE VAN VALIN AND CULTUROLOGY

Steve Van Valin is cofounder and CEO of Culturology, a consulting firm that boosts performance through workplace engagement. Their approach includes consulting on high-level strategy, ground-level tactics, and training solutions as a catalyst for positive change. Steve believes that in any organization the powerful combination of high performance accountability plus a highly-engaged workforce will proactively serve customer needs, ensure retained top talent, and build a solid foundation for sustainable success and innovation.

Steve got his first job in advertising sales for a radio station. There he learned the power of brainstorming, corporate culture shaping, and innovation by participating in a team that did all of these things really well. He then moved to Philadelphia, where he joined the affiliate sales and marketing team at a new television retail sales company called QVC.

QVC became an incredible entrepreneurial success story, which Steve attributes in part to its positive culture and philosophy, and the way they treated customers. Steve left the company after five years but was called back to lead the culture initiative at QVC, which was named "The QVC Difference."

After his success at QVC, Steve formed his own company called Culturology. The new venture was his opportunity to share his experiences and insights with other companies. He was especially interested in small start-ups that had not yet created their values.

Through Culturology, Steve helps companies shape the future of their culture—to build their culture by design, not by accident.

"I specialize specifically in innovation," Steve told me in an exclusive interview. "Innovation is the tail that wags the cultural dog. When a company is built on ideas and the ability to get them done, it's invigorating and engaging for people. Innovation can help shape the culture, and having a great culture can help drive innovation."

Steve believes that for a company to be more innovation-centric, you need to take a top-down, bottom-up approach. At the top, you need to articulate the vision for why innovation matters for a company. Having an aligned leadership team that has communicated that message is one of the key first steps. That is the top-down approach.

At the same time, the bottom-up approach means working at the grassroots level on giving people creative capacity. Steve helps employees and managers learn how to have powerful conversations with each other, brainstorm, conduct group meetings that help drive ideas, and raise their creative capacity. One key to success is giving people the confidence that they have the necessary abilities and intelligence to achieve higher goals. With confidence comes commitment and positive action.

Strengthening the top-down vision coupled with building the bottom-up creative capacity at the grassroots level is the best way to build an innovation-centric culture.

How much time and investment is necessary? It depends where the company is in terms of its creative capacity. If they have few ideas, abilities, or processes built into the system, it is going to take time to build. If they are shy on ideas but have a system to move ideas through, that will not take as long. Another scenario is a company that is really creative, but does not execute to the next level.

"I liken a company's culture to being sort of like a coral reef," Steve told me. "Just like a coral reef is built one tiny coral polyp at a time, a company culture is built one behavior at a time. Over time it forms something that becomes its own ecosystem and is actually incredibly beautiful and stunning to behold. Cultures form over time through those single behaviors, and it's not just something that you can instantly turn around. You can put a stake in the ground to say that you want to turn it around, but it's not going to happen overnight without tremendous discipline and a process to do that."

It is becoming a recognized fact that a positive company culture is not just a feel-good "soft" exercise; it will boost your bottom line. It will put bigger profits on your books. When people see that the company pursues a healthy way to operate, then work is more satisfying and fulfilling, and they feel more engaged coming to work. Employees want to get the most out of their work experience. This translates into innovative thinking, a passion for excellence, and a determination to do the very best job possible.

It all starts with leadership. "A leader must be a catalyst of innovation and drive progress in the organization," Steve told me. "When people see the CEO truly wants them to make progress and succeed, they'll jump through a brick wall for him or her."

PROFILE: JOE DENNY AT RAILCOMM

Do you think of railroads as being old-fashioned businesses that the digital age has left behind?

Do you imagine them as being relics of the twentieth century, when people used rotary phones and mile-long freight trains were guided by men waving flags?

Think again. While today's railroads still have the physical might of yore, they also have the brains of advanced computer guidance systems.

Along with six cofounders, Joe Denny, CEO of RailComm, struck gold in a niche market by developing sophisticated computer systems that control, monitor, and manage train yards from a centralized location. RailComm's expert solutions focus on improving operational efficiencies for the world's freight and transit rail industries. Their innovative systems have literally pulled outdated railroad yards into a new century of automation and computerization.

It all started in 1999, when Joe and his partners tackled an old problem: How to direct massive trains and freight cars onto the right sets of tracks. In those days, in the rail yards, workers manually maneuvered a switch machine (a mechanical device that has a spring in it and essentially moves the track from one position to another), allowing the trains to be guided onto one track or another. RailComm replaced the mechanical machines with remotely controlled automatic powered machines so a man in the control tower could use a computer to automatically route all of the required switches to form the route and move the train from point A to point B.

Their first job happened almost on a whim. One of their key customers said, "You know, it would be really great if you could embed your radio control capability into a power switch machine. Then we could use it for yard automation." It was the customer's idea, and Joe had the good sense to listen to it.

Electronic controls were in use on the main lines that ran between cities, but not in the more complex environment of the rail yard. Joe and his team worked with the suppliers of switch machines and built a microprocessor control board that would take in the data and interface to the mechanics within the switch box to actuate the machine. From the central control tower in the yard, a manager could route trains and rolling stock with the click of a mouse.

At RailComm, the process is just as important as the product. After looking at strategic goals for periods of one, two, or three years, the company plans around how they are going to achieve those goals. Everybody has their marching orders. It is not good enough to let employees remain alone in their silos and work on their marching orders. Everyone has to come back often as a team to make sure they are on target. The system allows the lowest person on the ladder—a technician or even the administrative assistant—to have a voice at the executive table.

"Growth is always the goal," Joe told me in an exclusive interview. "I incorporated much of the Toyota Management System, which makes everybody measurable and aware of the mission and goals. Each department uses *obeya* boards to make decisions and solve their own problems. (*Obeya* is a Japanese term that translates to "big room," or a place that can accommodate lots of ideas.) Issues they can't solve are submitted to the executive board, thus giving the front-line people a voice in the corner office."

To spread the word about his strategies for success, Joe formed a venture called ipPrimeMover. The company utilizes all the tools and techniques that he has experienced in the past and offers product development services to any company that creates or uses technology.

The company helps other firms develop technology products, and typically saves its clients at least 60 percent in development costs.

The idea came out of a program that Joe had introduced to RailComm. "I was searching for ways to change the culture of the company," Joe said, "even though it was a high performing company and everything was going great. We were constantly challenging the status quo."

"One of the areas that we had detected as a potential threat to the business was the fact that we had become hierarchical in our structure. We felt like we were losing that innovative edge that had gotten us to where we were."

"We got involved in a local program based in Berkeley, California, called Lean Startup. Steve Blank is one of the founders. It's all about how you start a new business. While the program is typically applied to startups, I firmly believe you can apply it at any stage of any company. The basic concept is that you're a startup. You have no money. You have an idea. You're trying to figure out how you get going."

The standard process had always been that you first write a business plan. Then you go shop the business plan, trying to get your initial investors on board.

Lean Startups turned all that upside down. They tell you not to write a business plan. Rather, they advise you to draw the *concept* of your business. The approach works particularly well for software businesses, because they have tools that allow them to quickly prototype their concepts.

Four of RailComm's key people attended the training for Lean Startup. The results were very positive. In fact, today the primary focus of RailComm is around Lean Startup and the new ideas that are generated from this core capability. As an existing company, RailComm was able to apply concepts that were designed for startups.

Perhaps that is one key to success—keep that startup mindset even as you grow into maturity.

PROFILE: MILLER INGENUITY'S STORY IS AMERICA'S STORY

Nothing could be closer to the heartland of American manufacturing than Miller Ingenuity, the company I have been privileged to lead since 1998. Based in Winona, Minnesota, Miller Ingenuity is an industry-leading supplier of mission critical systems for the global railroad industry.

The company was founded in 1948 by visionary, philanthropist, and inventor Rudy Miller. Rudy and his team invented and commercialized dozens of new and novel products that set the standard as industry firsts. By the early 1990s, the company, then known as Miller Felpax, held over 200 patents.

For 50 years Miller Felpax was very successful in selling its products exclusively to original equipment manufacturers (OEMs) of locomotives in the United States. The OEMs marketed and sold Miller's products to the end-user railroads. This channel strategy was perfect for many years because it created a situation where the company's products were specified—as they still are—on every new locomotive made in the United States.

In 1999, the company restructured its marketing channels and began distributing its products directly to the end-user railroads throughout the United States.

Within two years the new channel strategy greatly expanded the company and so weakened its biggest competitor that it sought to be acquired. Miller purchased that company in 2002.

Miller then entered the rail electronics market by introducing a highway crossing signal that, unlike most crossing signals in the industry at the time, did not use an incandescent bulb; rather it used high-efficiency and long-lasting light emitting diodes. The company quickly became the industry's leading supplier of LED highway crossing signals, and soon captured the largest installed base in the world.

By 2010, the company had acquired several more of its competitors and had expanded significantly, including direct distribution to railroads in international markets.

In 2012, the company rebranded its name from Miller Felpax to Miller Ingenuity to better reflect its capabilities as a company oriented toward technology solutions. It also entered the rail radio communications market with the purchase of an industry leading radio communications supplier.

In 2014 Miller Ingenuity opened the Creation Station, the first Google-like campus in a factory in the state of Minnesota. The Creation Station cultivates innovation from the inside out as a state-of-the-art collaborative space where Miller Ingenuity team members—both blue and white collar—and our customers convene to develop, discuss, exchange, and nurture ideas both big and small that can benefit the company, our customers, or the community at large. In fact, employees are encouraged and expected to spend 20 percent of their time there.

A first-of-its-kind dedicated ideation space in the manufacturing industry in Minnesota, the Creation Station serves Miller Ingenuity's mission to apply "maximum ingenuity to customer needs, problems, or opportunities." In a business landscape where billion-dollar technology companies such as Google and Apple dominate the headlines for innovation and are revered for their creativity-supporting cultures, Miller Ingenuity's Creation Station makes a bold statement:

> Fostering collaborative, creative thinking among employees can benefit every industry and every company, no matter its size or how long it's been in business.

The Creation Station means more than business. It is also a place for socialization, sharing, and relaxation, where employees at all levels come together anytime with each other and with customers. There is plenty of space for meetings big or small, with tables, chairs, and booths for small groups or one-on-one interactions. Its large, bright windows play off the Creation Station's invitation: "Always open." Around the clock it is ready for a meal at the Caboose Cafe, a game of pool, researching an idea, conversations that lead to surprising inventions, savvy engineering, and reliable execution. The spirit of innovation never closes at Miller Ingenuity.

But the Creation Station is only a room. It has no magical powers to generate ideas. As Randy Skarlupka, our vice president of manufacturing, said, "The magic is in the employees."

I would agree and even take that one step further, and say the magic is in the culture. In our case, a culture of innovation.

Miller Ingenuity's culture of innovation accelerated in 2015 when it launched two more revolutionary industry firsts. One was the DuraForce Fastener system, a unique product that solved a critical problem that had plagued the rail industry for decades. The second was Miller Ingenuity's most audacious initiative yet: a line of high-technology products designed to prevent fatal railroad accidents.

I believe that if every manufacturer were to identify and embrace those innovations that bring it more value, the manufacturing industry could capitalize on the huge opportunity before it with the shifting global economy. By nurturing a company culture where employees are encouraged and enabled to generate, explore, and evaluate fresh ideas, any manufacturer can out-think, out-innovate, and out-perform foreign competition.

ELEVEN

We Did It Once, We Can Do It Again

One American industry after another has gone the way of lower cost and offshore competition. It seems like every day you hear of more jobs being lost to the Chinese. And since the media relishes bad news, it is unlikely you will ever hear of jobs coming back to the United States.

That is, unless you go looking.

In this book, you have read some inspirational stories from the heartland. Basic industry companies that have pulled themselves up by the bootstraps, taken huge risks, and pulled off spectacular comebacks. These stories are proof positive that if we did it once before, we can do it again. In the next chapter, I will offer my final thoughts and a personal prescription for comeback success.

The United States is the greatest country on the planet—or at least that is what people like to say. And although we still have the world's largest economy, in terms of manufacturing, banking, and other sectors, we are in danger of becoming a second-rate country to China. I can see no upside in losing our place as the world's super-economic power, only the downside.

The mainstay of American economic power, and therefore its national security, has always been its technology and manufacturing. If we continue to lose manufacturing parity to other countries, America will be in economic and eventually national security peril.

It is not enough to be optimistic and upbeat about the future of manufacturing. Many people tout the "great American manufacturing comeback."

And while there has been encouraging evidence of that, much more needs to be done. We need to take action. Each and every leader in American manufacturing needs to take action—*right now.*

Several well-meaning organizations and associations have dedicated themselves to the revitalization of American manufacturing. Most of them concern themselves with U.S. manufacturing policy and how the government is either enhancing or destroying the sector. These organizations play a useful role in influencing the government. But—and this is a big "but"—they do not *make* anything. They educate, inform, illuminate, and sometimes influence government and manufacturing executives alike, but that does not move the GDP one iota. So if you are relying on these organizations to save American manufacturing, it is never going to happen. Only *you* can do that in your role as a manufacturing leader. You need to ignore government policy and focus on the job at hand, which is making every widget better than the widget before.

During the Great Recession of 2007–2009, I formed a CEO mastermind group. The idea was to band together and share ideas and tactics so we could all get through the downturn in one piece. During our discussions, one CEO kept on insisting we talk about government policies. He wanted to complain about how the government caused the recession (I guess he never heard of the business cycle) and how it continued to delay the recovery with bad economic policy.

I am not sure, but I think he actually believed little ole' Mr. Manufacturer could have an impact on governmental policy. He was deluding himself into believing that *complaining* about government policy was the same thing as *doing* something about the mess his company was in. It was not. He forgot the first rule of business: focus on what you *can* control, not what you *can't.*

As a leader of a manufacturing business, you need to focus on what you can do to improve your operation, not what the government should do to improve it for you. And if every manufacturing business in America improved itself by even 1 percent, the overall impact on the health of manufacturing, and the U.S. economy, would be staggering.

A mere 1 percent is within the power of you and your company to achieve. A mere 1 percent is within every manufacturer's power. All you have to do is decide to do it. Sounds simple, doesn't it? Well, maybe it is, but *how* do you do it? While many of the answers to that can be found in this book, you can also find answers by looking to the past.

Let's start by taking a look at the early settlers in America. The people who crossed the Great Plains in wagons, floated down rivers on rafts, and staked out claims in uncharted territories. They were a hardy bunch, to be sure. Their very lives depended upon The 7 Values of Ingenuity™. They did not call it that, or even necessarily recognize it as such, but that is how they survived. And how this country became great.

The settlers banded together to form a tight bond as a community. They did not backstab each other and vie for the boss's attention. They stuck together like glue. The members put the community before the individual. The community was more important than any one person. That is how they survived in such a harsh environment. That is how they survived one natural disaster after another.

Fast-forward to modern times natural disasters. In 2013, Hurricane Sandy nearly wiped out IceStone, a sustainable countertop manufacturer, for the second time. The financial crisis of 2008 had nearly wiped IceStone out the first time.

As I recounted earlier in this book, IceStone is an incredible story in perseverance and ingenuity, and a perfect example of the "settler's fighting spirit."

When these pioneers built homes and bridges they did not do "just enough to get by." They did not have to measure quality defects—there simply *were none*. They could not afford to settle for anything less than excellence. And over time, the standards of excellence were instilled in them and their descendants.

They did not go off on their own and try to outdo each other. That was a sure formula for disaster and perhaps even death. They did not withhold information from each other to make another member look bad. "Settler politics" did not exist. No, they bonded together in highly effective teams. And they did not need some human resource guy to teach them how to work in teams; they learned it on their own as a matter of necessity. These life-or-death survival skills became ingrained in them as "the way things are done around here."

Their leaders were not looking out for their careers; they were looking out for their teams and their people.

I know what you are thinking: "Different deal, different time. Their lives were on the line, while my people just want to make it to five o'clock. It's easy to work in teams when your life depends upon it. When you work at a mundane job, day in and day out ..."

You are right, but that is not my point. My point is this:

Once upon a time, American workers had the values and spirit of the settlers.

Today, many still do.

A perfect story to illustrate that fighting settlers' spirit is Northern Woolen Mills. As you know, one of the industries that was lost long ago to foreigners was the wool industry. In the 1940s, the United States was ranked number five in the world in wool production. By 2013 we had plummeted to number 11. Seems like most companies in the United States simply gave up on the industry and let it go.

But at least one brought it back. Against all odds.

PROFILE: STEPHENIE ANDERSON, NORTHERN WOOLEN MILLS

Fosston, Minnesota, is as heartland as heartland gets. A town in the northwestern corner of the state, its population is a mere 1,500. While it may not sound like a good place to start a wool industry revolution, that is exactly what Northern Woolen Mills has done. The company opened its doors in December 2013, after CEO Stephenie Anderson and her team had cobbled together $755,000 to buy the assets needed to open the mill. There was a steep learning curve; in some cases, the only processes and procedures to run the machines were available on YouTube, in Spanish.

And now the company produces 100 pounds of yarn a day. Pretty good for an industry that is having a near death experience, wouldn't you say?

For Anderson, an important key is employee empowerment. "We have a responsibility as owners," she told me, "to make sure our staff can take charge. I consider that we have done our job when they can take care of everything by themselves."

As for competing with Chinese manufacturers, Anderson says, "Where you're buying from in China and India, those people pay their workers *cents*. They pay six dollars a week for their employees, where I pay real people wages, and that's a challenge. When I'm working with these mid-size companies, they can buy yarn for five dollars a pound because they're not paying for labor and stuff. I can sometimes come close and sometimes I'm a lot more. Sometimes I'm twenty dollars a pound, but that's another challenge. You have to add value, because you're not going to get there with price alone."

Too many companies have lost the settlers' spirit. Their employees just do not have it. And it was not their fault. It was management's fault. That means it was *your* fault. How did this happen?

During the Industrial Revolution, hand production was replaced or augmented with automation (as it existed at the time) and the use of better factor inputs, such as steam power and coal in place of wood. That was the start of the century-long belief that machines and processes are better than, and more important than, people. And when Frederick Taylor introduced the Scientific Theory, the settlers' work ethic and community spirit was beaten out of them and they were told and trained to act like automatons. And because it actually worked for a while (okay, maybe a long while), it reinforced the belief that people are really only small cogs in the industrial wheel. In fact, Taylor actually had quite a condescending attitude toward "the workers," often calling them stupid. If you know anything about expectancy theory, you can imagine what that attitude did to creativity.

Then we sought to marginalize the human element even further by chasing cheaper labor first to the southern United States, then to Mexico, then to Asia. The philosophy behind this was the same as "Taylorism": We don't need the workers' minds, only their hands. And the cheapest hands we can find at that.

The gains did not last long.

Exploiting labor was central to U.S. manufacturing's rise to preeminence in the world. *But now it is central to its demise.* This is a very important point. Too many leaders are still using the same labor exploitation model. Too many managers (you cannot really call them "leaders") still tolerate, in fact even expect, employees to check their brains at the door. It is no wonder that they do.

PROFILE: DOUGLAS WOODS, AMT

Douglas Woods is the president of the Association for Manufacturing Technology (AMT). AMT represents and supports manufacturing technology in the United States and its members, who build, design, sell, and provide service to continuously advancing technologies. Located in Virginia, AMT provides specific business and expansive global support, as well as intelligence systems and evaluation. AMT actively communicates the significance of policies, research and innovation programs, and educational proposals to build tomorrow's "smartforce."

A lifelong manufacturing guy, Doug's grandfather owned a tool and die manufacturing company in Rochester, New York. He started Alliance in 1947 with nine other partners and he grew it into a $100 million manufacturing company by 1979, at which point it was acquired by Gleason Corporation, which is one of the biggest gear equipment manufacturing companies in the world, also a Rochester company. The family's life centered around the manufacturing facility, and at age fifteen, Doug went to work at the shop. Every summer he worked in the tool shop, and went through a tool and die apprenticeship.

Doug worked in different divisions of Alliance, which included standard tool and die, precision machining, mold making division, a metal stamping division, leak testing stands, an automation division. His experience was across a wide range of manufacturing technologies, working with tool makers, mold makers, automation controls, and electrical engineering people.

When Gleason acquired Alliance, he then got a chance to work at a much bigger corporation. He worked within their enterprise, and traveled to some of their international facilities to learn and help them with their quality programs. Doug had a dual degree in finance and statistics before he went back for a manufacturing technology degree, and he did statistical quality control, control charts, and how to do preventative quality versus doing failure mode quality.

Eventually Doug got to run his own company in Rochester. It was an $8 million tool and die company that he turned into a $50 million automation company. It took 16 years of developing different parts of the company and selling off divisions. They had a thin film technology, a mold technology division, and divisions were built up and then spun off, allowing the company to focus on the automation business. Doug learned what it takes to grow a company from a small-town tool and die company into a major player fulfilling first tier automotive contracts worth $20 million.

Doug then learned what it means to fail. After taking a company that was almost bankrupt and turning it into a thriving enterprise, the firm had some major projects that they had built for a couple of automotive customers at a time when those automotive customers were having their own difficulties and going through their own Chapter 11s. The company had equipment that they could not get off the floor and delivered to the end customer. These were big, $15 million systems.

Their bank decided that manufacturing highly specialized equipment that was not sellable to anybody else was a bad investment, and they closed off the company's lines of capital, which forced Doug to close the business.

Doug learned from his experience. As Doug told me in an exclusive interview, "Most of the successful people whom I've met have had their failures somewhere along the line. These failures hardened them into figuring out how to build a better mousetrap based on what didn't go well with something they did previously. I mortgaged my house to take over an eight-million-dollar tool and die company that was nearly bankrupt, and the things that made me successful doing that are the things that made me unsuccessful with a different type of company fifteen years later."

It is a valuable lesson that some of the same strategies that brought his company success later blinded him to a new set of challenges. To get the company on its feet, they focused—rightly—on core competencies. They eliminated what they were not good at doing. They put systems in place, and developed repetitive projects as opposed to doing something new every time. They figured out how to leverage key structures or elements so that they could repeat the cell again and just modify the fixturing or the tool handling so that they did not have so much white paper every time being created. Those were the keys to success, along with building up and leveraging his people to be the best people at attaining that. That brought them success.

What killed them at the other end was that they operated as if they were a half-billion-dollar company trying to lead technology. They were one of the first people to try 3D technology back in the late 1990s. For a little $40 million tool company, some of these reaches in R&D were really a little bit outside the bounds of their ability to finance those as part of their normal operating business model. They lost their focus on the bedrock principle that "cash is king." The balance sheet was not strong enough to support leading edge technologies.

If you do not build a very sound financial and business plan that is equally as important as your strategic and technical and innovative plan, it is not going to work. The two things have to be glued together. You cannot just have a great innovative idea and think that automatically the financial plan is going to follow in behind it reaping you rewards. It does not work that way.

The other big thing was that the company was 99 percent automotive. While they covered a lot of different types of people in automotive, they were all automotive. If the automotive sector went down, they were going to feel the pinch. The thought process at the time was, "Well, automotive is big enough that we can be diversified enough," but the reality is you need to be insulated from a particular market segment in order to execute a strategy like that.

Doug learned that it would have been better to be a little bit smaller, not go after every big job, and put a little bit more margin to the bottom line instead of taking on extra volume to run up their revenue number. It is better to run up your margin number, not just your revenue number.

They do not teach this stuff in business school. You have to learn these things in real life. Some people have a board of directors or perhaps their bank or someone else they are working with who helps them navigate those waters, so while they have similar trips and falls, they have a guiding solution externally to keep them from going too far off the rails.

If you are a small company, find the right advisers who do not just say "yes" to you, but are truly giving you that Dutch uncle kind of discussion where they can say, "I think you're crazy, that's not what you should be doing. You need to rethink your strategy." You should surround yourself with those kinds of people. You need to have those things in place. The right kind of bank partner and the right type of board or advisers can help guide you no matter your company size.

As Doug told me, "As leaders, we get up there at the top and we think we know it all and we don't really need anybody to tell us anything, and sometimes the people whom we need to tell us the most are the people whom we need to hear from. One of the best traits of an effective leader is that they're a very good communicator. They're a very good persuader. They're really good at making their point and making others believe that's the right path and that's where you want to go."

"You're going to get people passionate about following that path. While that's a good thing and it's necessary as a leader to get your folks doing that, sometimes you can get to the point where when your people are trying to explain a contrary position, you're using those tools and those gifts persuade people out of a position you should be spending more time listening to. Sometimes the gift of getting you where you need to be as a leader can also be a detriment if you're not careful about using your ears a little bit more often."

CEOs tend to latch onto an idea and go running with it; and when they think it is the right thing to do, they do not stop as often as they should to look at it closely and say, "Is it really the right thing to do?" When they conclude it is the right thing to do, they go 110 percent.

While closing the company was a painful experience, Doug's bank helped ease the process. They made it an orderly liquidation and worked with the company to try to complete as many of the contracts as they could, and pay off as many suppliers as they could.

"I sat down with the employees," said Doug. "I brought them all into the cafeteria and said, 'Look, here's the situation. We're going to have to close the company. Everyone's going to lose their job, including me, of course. Here's a sheet with your name and a layoff date on it. Unfortunately, those jobs that are least necessary in getting product shipped out the door and money collected are the ones we're going to have to let go first, with the last ones being installation, service, and warranty. You can see your name with the date next to it and that's the last date that we can pay you. Then you'll get your vacation or severance or whatever we owe you at that point."

"I also explained to them, 'Look, I understand you all have families to take care of and other things. You know you're going to be losing your job at that point. If you find a better opportunity and you just need to leave for your family, to do what you've got to do, you do what you have to do. Take the job, we'll figure out how to cover for you.' "

Out of 150 employees, nobody left before their layoff date.

That is the key to building a strong company. Anyone can buy the same equipment that you use. Anybody can use the supply base that you use. Anyone can have the facility that you operate out of. The differentiating factor for the business at the end of the day is the people at the business. As Doug told me, "It's all about integrating those people in such a way that you're doing things for them, they're doing things for you, and you're creating that ability to use the minds of all those people driving the business forward, collectively, to really make a powerhouse."

Passion, Pride, Family, and Fun

"I think as unfortunate as that situation was," said Doug, "when you create a core organization that's got passion and pride, you can see the value. We built four core principles at the company: Passion, pride, family, and fun."

If you are not passionate about what you are doing, you should not be there. If you do not have pride in what you shipped and delivered and executed, you should not be there. You have to take care of your family first, but your second family are those people whom you work with every day that you are spending a lot of your waking moments with. You have to be covering for those people and working with them and looking out for them. And lastly, if you do not have some fun while you are doing this—well, life is too short, and you should rethink how you do what you do.

The core principles in a company are the things that differentiate you and create that culture that allows one company with the same equipment as some other company to do something different and better. You build a culture not by default but by design.

What Doug did sounds a lot like The 7 Values of Ingenuity™, doesn't it?

At the time he closed the company, Doug was on the board of AMT. He then had an opportunity to take over and run a company for a friend of his in Rochester. Three years later, he put his hat in the ring for the job of president of AMT. He was hired in 2009, and he's been there since then.

As Doug said to me, "If you're a manufacturing guy, being president of AMT is a dream job. You get to touch the entire industry. You get to work with some of the best technology companies, big and small, in the United States. You get to see what they're doing around the world with pure associations and what they're doing developing the technology around the world. It's really a unique opportunity if you're a manufacturing centered person like I am."

As opposed to trying to run AMT like a typical industry association, Doug treats it more like what you would do if you were running a company that needed to be responsive to the marketplace and delivered products and the services that would help the membership.

As president, Doug helped AMT develop three specific areas to focus on:

1. Innovation in R&D
2. Global competitiveness
3. Building an educated smartforce

Then they put different policies that members could do under those things. As Doug said, "Our members are trying to run their businesses every day. We try to give them, in a very simple and easy to use manner that they can leverage, a tool they didn't know they should have. The business intelligence platform is one of those things that is like that, so that's where we focus."

Looking at the Future

"Manufacturing in the United States has been on about a four-year, extremely positive roll," said Doug. "I see nothing to change that, and the reason that it's different now than ever in the past is because manufacturing is becoming the 'in vogue' thing. 3D has unbelievable practical applications, and as far as manufacturing goes, it's created a generation of kids who are actually manufacturing, even if they don't know it."

The whole maker movement, maker fairs, shapeway—all that has taken kids who normally would not have been involved in manufacturing and are involved with manufacturing now. If you can design it, you can make it, and then put things together on your own to have your own little products. You could launch what you want, when you want it, and where you want it. It is the perfect credo to anybody in manufacturing—that is what you want at the end of the day. Now you have all the tools to go do that and it is making manufacturing hip, cool, and new. Data and analytics and things like augmented reality, adaptive learning systems, and collaborative robotics are going to be the key parts. Automation sensors and what drives manufacturing in the next decade or two, are areas we excel at in the United States.

"We might not be the best at creating the next three-axis gantry mill machine," Doug told me. "We've been there, done that. Maybe we gave up some of that market share in some cases of traditional areas, but when you look at a lot of these new technologies and leveraging them into traditional technology and leveraging the production solution, we lead in that. We're great at that and we're going to continue to excel worldwide because of that."

Final Thoughts: It's the Employee, Stupid

YOU NEED A NEW RELATIONSHIP WITH YOUR EMPLOYEES

The old attitudes will not work anymore. Rather than exploit, today's leaders need to *capitalize* on and *nurture* the human spirit. They need to create the conditions to let employees be like the settlers again. To let them do what they want to do, which is to be productive and satisfied in the place they spend most of their adult lives. People *want* to do good work. We just do not *let* them, with our silly rules and procedures, and our cultures that are messy at best and destructive at worst. And then we try to "manage" them. Do this, do that. Do what you are told and nothing else.

I travel extensively and see evidence of the "do this" management style all the time. I was once at a hotel in Buenos Aires and noticed the cleaning people followed a checklist. Do this, do that. The checklist dictated exactly what the automaton was to do. But by virtue of dictating what must be done it left no room for unexpected circumstances. It left no room for creativity or inventiveness. In fact, if the cleaning people saw something that they thought should be done, they probably were not even *allowed* to do it. How can the hotel expect people who are imprisoned by a checklist to feel empowered and satisfied in their work life? How much value does the hotel lose by treating the cleaning people like kindergarteners?

I know what you are saying: Without rules and checklists, anarchy will rule the workplace.

If you have a culture by default and not by design, then this is true—it will.

And you say, these people have to be "managed." Well, I have bad news for you. You are not managing them now; your checklists are. And there is no management of others, only self-management. You cannot manage or control anyone.

I have created many businesses in developing countries. Every time I entered into one, people would say I was crazy because I would not be able to manage and "control" a business halfway across the world. In fact, I have had businesses that were separated by as few as 20 and as much as 8,000 miles. And you know what? The so-called control issues were always the same.

Control is an illusion.

There is no control—only *influence*.

You cannot control anything. But you can influence *everything*.

How much value is your company losing with "checklist" management? How many times do your employees see something that would clearly reduce cost but the checklist forbids they try it? How many times do your employees go home at night and tell their spouses how stupid you are because you will not let people close to the action make things better when they clearly know better than you?

YOU NEED TO NURTURE THE HUMAN SPIRIT IN THE WORKPLACE

The salvation of American manufacturing is in the human spirit. Many societal and technology trends have influenced the need for employees to be free spirits again. Their lower level needs on the Maslow hierarchy have been met. They long for something more. And they long for it in the workplace.

These trends are accelerating. Tomorrow's employee will long for more than today's. I cannot tell you how many leaders I know who expect and even demand that millennials act like baby boomers. They are in denial as to the realities of this accelerating trend. It cannot be stopped. You should not even want to stop it. You should enable and facilitate it. That is how you win in the marketplace. Especially against China, a country that is likely not to allow any "human spirit" nonsense in the workplace.

But you cannot create the human spirit in the workplace. You can only *unleash* it. So how do you unleash human spirit at work?

I can give you some guiding principles.

Put People First and Profits Will Follow

This is not some Pollyannaish ideal. It is a very practical, proven principle that produces spectacular results. But before you think it means you should let the human resource people run the business into "happy days are here again," that is not what it means. Human resource people will always want employees to be "happy." But happy employees are not necessarily high performing employees; they are only happy. Happy is not your primary goal. I am not saying people who get their needs met in the workplace will not be happy. They probably will, but that is not your goal. It is a by-product of a much deeper sense of personal satisfaction.

No, what you want is what I like to call Cirque du Soleil-like employees. And what is that? Creative, high-energy people who come to work every day all jazzed up to perform on the very edge and be better than they were yesterday. Imagine the performance your company could have if every single employee were like that?

You will not get Cirque-like employees if you do not put them first. And it also means that anyone who cannot be or does not want to be Cirque-like cannot stay. That is the other side of the people first equation.

Imagine this: You are a high-wire performer and the guy who is supposed to catch you is having a bad day. And he has a bad attitude to boot. In fact, he is not as good as you would like him to be. He is sloppy and inconsistent. How long will you stay in the performing group if something is not done about this guy? It is the same way in the workplace. If the goal is to maintain an on-the-edge high-wire act, you cannot afford anything less than ultra-competence from every single employee.

Is this easy to do? No it is not. Once you have established such an elite group of people, you have to continually prune the tree because it is inevitable someone will sneak in on you who does not belong. Or as often as not, for unknowable reasons, a high performer decides he does not want to be that anymore and just checks out. And once they have checked out, shame on you for letting that happen. But take it from me, once it happens, you cannot check them back in again. You have to let them go.

Put Family First and Profits Will Follow

What does that mean? Let me give you some examples. When anyone on my team has a family crisis I always tell them the same thing: "Take care of your [spouse, parent, child] and don't worry about your job. Take all the time you need and don't rush to get back. You'll still get paid. Don't even think about us. *Put your family first.*"

In any company I ever ran, not only did I consider employees as part of the company family, but their families too. Call it extended corporate families if you will. For all you hard-nosed businesspeople out there, think of it this way: When a child of an employee is seriously ill, there is no way the employee can be productive. Forcing them to work (because in all too many cases, they do not get paid if they don't) creates only resentment and increases the potential for quality problems and costly mistakes.

So why not treat them like family and let them have the time off, with pay and without restrictions? You would not believe the goodwill and loyalty such a position creates.

"But," you say, "they'll take advantage of my generosity and only come back to work when they're good and ready."

There you go again, thinking like Frederick Taylor. If you have hired the right people, you do not have to worry about that. In fact, if you have hired the right people, they will feel badly for taking any time off at all, let alone too much time. They pretty much police themselves. You do not have to.

Put Profits First and Profits Will Follow; Put Profits Last and No Profits Will Follow

This sounds like an oxymoron but you would not believe how many companies focus on everything else but profit. If you looked at the number of goals and objectives in the average middle market company, I bet you would find they number in the hundreds. And most of them would not have profit in the goal. You would find quality goals, delivery goals, inventory goals and all kinds of goals that not only do not have the word *profit* in them, but are not even quantifiable.

These organizations are following an endless loop of activity. Do the activity, finish the activity. Do the activity again. They are focused on doing things, not getting results. And they think it is all good. After all, quality goals are good, right? Improving this and improving that is good, right?

It is better to focus on nothing than the wrong thing. Let me repeat that: It is better to focus on nothing than the wrong thing. Why? Focusing on the wrong thing lulls the organization to sleep with a false sense of security. And how can you tell if it is the wrong thing? If it does not add profit to the organization, it is the wrong thing. It is as simple as that.

This is where many people tell me it is insane to think everyone in the company should add profit.

I disagree. To me, it is insane to have anyone on the payroll who *does not* add profit.

If you are in a for-profit business, never forget that *goal one is profit.*

Secondary goals—and keep these to an absolute minimum—must be in direct support of goal one. And everyone in the organization should pledge allegiance to the flag of profit. There should be no mistake in anyone's mind that increasing profit is the number one goal.

Skeptics will say that these principles are incompatible. They will say that unleashing the human spirit will not lead to more profit, only to more happy people. They will say that making profit goal one will turn people against the organization.

But the fact is, having one without the other *will* result in what the skeptics claim. Unleashing the human spirit *without directing it toward profit* will result in happy people but not more profit. In fact, this will result in less profit due to the cost of unleashing the human spirit (and yes, there is a cost to do this). Pledging allegiance to profit without unleashing the human spirit leads to resentment and dissatisfaction, which results in less profit.

It is essential to do both.

Think of it this way: We cannot be one big happy family unless there is plenty of food on the table. And we will not have plenty of food on the table unless we are one big happy family.

These seemingly opposing principles and their practices are difficult for most leaders to embrace. But embrace them they must if we are to take back American manufacturing from the onslaught of the Chinese. In fact, this is our last and best competitive weapon against the Chinese. They will never embrace the human spirit. The Chinese way is to subjugate the will of the individual to the will of the State.

That is how we win against them. And that is how we fix what went wrong and how we make it right.

Remember the words of Donald Douglas: "Free men can out-produce slaves." Are your employees truly free to rise to their highest potential? Or are they slaves to antiquated ideas and systems? As a leader, you have the power to free your people from the chains of bureaucracy and unleash their full potential for greater pride, and productivity, and profits.

It is your choice.

Make it today.

Index